FIFTY
TYPEFACES
THAT
CHANGED
THE
WORLD

DESIGN
MUSEUM

FIFTY
TYPEFACES
THAT
CHANGED
THE
WORLD

JOHN L
WALTERS

conran
OCTOPUS

FIFTY TYPEFACES

FIFTY TYPEFACES

Take a look at the page in front of you. Not at what I've written, but at the way it looks – the neat rows of typesetting, each horizontal line evenly separated from the lines above and/or below; each word carefully spaced from the next; each letter pleasingly close to, yet separate from, its neighbour. That's typography.

Now take a look at each individual letter. These are all taken from a typeface called DM Schulbuch, a typeface made for the Design Museum. Each 'a' is exactly like all the others, as is each 'g'. It is partly this mechanical precision (compared to the variations of hand lettering) that makes type what it is. A harmonious collection of characters – letters plus numbers, punctuation marks, currency symbols and so on – has been crafted into a hard-working typeface.

The typeface exerts an influence on the reader. It conveys a mood, or personality that can affect the experience of reading. Yet the everyday demands of reading mean that the art of the type designer is self-effacing – people tend to notice a bad or unfamiliar typeface more often than they point out good or familiar faces.

For more than five centuries, type designers have expended long hours crafting personal versions of the letters of the alphabet. Small changes – the thickness of a curve, the angle of a stroke – make big differences to the look of a page set in that type. Like musical instrument makers, type designers have no control over repertoire or performers. Apart from a typeface's intrinsic aesthetic merits, there are many factors, including luck, fashion and timing, that affect the way in which a face is used, the context in which it is read, and whether it snarls or sings its message.

Each of the faces featured in this little book has a story, whether it's the story of its design, its use or the reputation it has acquired. And each story is a tribute to the ingenious, talented designers and craftspeople, many of them anonymous, who have given us this delightful feast of letterforms...

Proof of early wooden type made for the London Underground typeface, now called Johnston Sans, with handwritten notes by its designer, Edward Johnston, c.1916.

Page 2: Ampersand from a nineteenth-century wood typeface. From the collection at the Hamilton Wood Type & Printing Museum, Two Rivers, Wisconsin.

zʎxʍʌ

aɥᴉjʞlɯnɹs

obdɔǝbdqo 8

ODBEFNIJKLMN

PQURSTVWC X

GKKS W & Y X Z X

BHKQURAILWAY

Revised 4–12 March.
rejected HWSJW (×A) renewed
New NXKKSB added. Z etc

Edward Johnston, Ditchling, Sussex
1st Drawings. F.b.F. 1916.

Photo-litho of preliminary & unfinished EJ drawings of spring 1916 (Reduced v. scale)

The first large-scale project to use type was the 42-line Gutenberg Bible (c.1455). The type was based on the lettering used by monks to copy manuscripts. Though Johannes Gutenberg's revolutionary use of moveable type supplanted the time-consuming labour of scribes with a faster mechanical process, its aim was to provide a legible alternative to the handwritten book. This kind of letter is termed blackletter or 'broken script'.

Though 'roman' types soon emerged as a more ubiquitous form, blackletter types were used in Germany for several centuries: at the time of Luther, blackletter typefaces symbolized the liberation of Protestant Germans from the Roman Catholic Church (c.1517).

In German-speaking countries, roman (often preferred for scientific texts) and blackletter types rubbed along nicely until 1933, when the Nazis declared that all official materials must be printed in Fraktur, including the new pseudo-Gothic fonts that typesetters nicknamed *Schaftstiefelgrotesk* ('jackboot grotesks'). In 1941 the Nazis made a U-turn: Martin Bormann forbade the use of Fraktur, explaining that 'Gothic' letters were Jewish (though his motives were practical, given the Third Reich's need to print propaganda in the countries it intended to invade and occupy.

Nonetheless, blackletter typefaces – which include Goudy Text, Old English and more postmodern versions such as Fetish and Bastard – have remained popular.

Blackletter characters, in their myriad forms, have many (often contradictory) cultural associations, from the Gutenberg Bible (top left) to metal bands (such as Motörhead and Judas Priest); from newspaper mastheads (*Chicago Tribune*, *Le Monde*, *Daily Telegraph*) to alcohol, antique shops and hospitality.

FIRST ROMAN TYPE
Venetian revolution

Nicolas [Nicholas] Jenson

The first roman type of any significance appears to have been established by Nicolas Jenson (c.1430–80). Jenson was a Frenchman who had been sent to Mainz in 1448 by the French king Charles VII to find out about Gutenberg's innovations. In 1470 he set up a workshop in Venice and became a prolific printer of Classical works set in type that is still regarded as a model for the roman type of today. The upper-case letters follow the capitals used in Roman inscriptions while the lower case comes from handwriting with a broad-edged pen, a form called 'humanist'.

Jenson had been an apprentice at the Royal Mint in Paris, and the documents that survived after his death suggest that he cast type in adjustable moulds using copper matrices struck with steel punches. This way of making and printing type – letterpress – would dominate publishing for almost the next five centuries.

The influence of Jenson's roman letters resurfaced in the late nineteenth century when William Morris designed a revival called Golden, intended for use in his three-volume edition of *The Golden Legend* (1892). This stimulated renewed interest in Jenson's era as designers sought inspiration for new typefaces. US designer Bruce Rogers also discovered Jenson as part of his quest for the 'Holy Grail' of type, which resulted in his typeface Centaur (1914–29).

More contemporary versions of Jenson's type include Christian Schwartz's Houston (2003; for the *Houston Chronicle*), Tobias Frere-Jones's Hightower (1994; for the *AIGA Journal*), Robert Slimbach's Adobe Jenson (1995) and Jim Parkinson's lettering for the *Rolling Stone* masthead (1977), which he has described as 'Nicolas Jenson on acid'.

Detail of a page of Pliny's *Historia naturale*, printed in Venice by Nicolas Jenson in 1476, from a collection of enlarged photos of early type collected by William Morris for use in designing the type of the Kelmscott Press. Jenson's type can be recognized by its angled lower-case 'e'.

abcdefghijk123
LMNO,.£%*"

erano gente dipreg

Tucti questi facce

unga mosseno efi

ote sforzo italmar

ati &fossi inpiu lu

ne uscire ne etra

nan fra lemura de

euano apistoia: P

o nelpontificato

'THE ALDINE ITALIC'
Inclined to save space

1501
Aldus Manutius &
Francesco Griffo

Early in the sixteenth century the Italian printer Aldus Manutius (1449–1515) commissioned the punchcutter Francesco Griffo (1450–1518) to cut a typeface that would represent written scripts more closely. Hence the term 'italic' – the letters were intended to look like Italian handwriting.

The 'Aldine italic' was welcomed both for its elegance and its economy. Aldus used this new typeface to print the entire text of an edition of Virgil (1501) in the new pocket-sized octavo format. Venetian publishers were obliged to pursue a more economical approach after the collapse of the credit market in 1500, and Griffo's slimline design was intended to permit more words in less space. Aldus's *libri portatiles* were the Penguin paperbacks of their day.

The new type was quickly copied and adopted by printers elsewhere in Europe, but it was not until the end of the following century that the italic face was used the way typographers use it today – for emphasis, or as a means to distinguish book titles, works of art or foreign-language words.

Aldus Manutius is remembered as one of the great Venetian printers. In 1499 he published the illustrated *Hypnerotomachia Poliphili*, which used one size of roman type (now revived as Poliphilus, which designer Derek Birdsall calls 'the most readable typeface, ever') throughout.

A page from the pocket-sized edition of poems by Johannes Aurelius Augurellus, printed by Aldus Manutius in 1505 using the new, allegedly space-saving italic typeface cut by Francesco Griffo. Courtesy Amsterdam University Library.

Maius onus super inducis, quam ferre tuis est
Par humeris, qui multa diu tam magna tulerūt.
Nec subit interea quā nanum è marmore littus
Spectare, ut tuto ualeas te condere portu,
Ni semel incipias illhuc torquere carinam ·
Quod si forte roges ubinam locus ille quietis :
Montibus his possim tibi respondere tuismet
Innixus uerbis, et re quoq; nanq; salubri
Temperie coeli præstant : ut qui pote nunc te
Tam cito reddiderint sanum recteq; ualentem ·
Suppetit hic etiam cunctarum copia rerum ·
Est et Amoenus ager secessibus undiq; septus :
Mens ubi turbarum cumulum deponere possit ·
Nó tamen hic quanuis tot rerū est præditus usu :
Excutiet solitas ægro de pectore curas :
Est animus nisi cópositus : qui se quoq; dignum
Ipse loco faciat : qui clauum dirigat, et qui
Hæc subeat sospes plenis semel hostia uelis ;

TRYPHONI CHABRIELO PATRI
CIO VENETO. QVICVM EA
ridet, quæ uulgus admiratur ·

SERMO · IIII ·

      Ic tuus huc aditus fuerat mihi Ca ⁓
h   rior auro
Care Tryphon, abitus uerū est insuauis, et ipsa

GARAMOND
A two-faced story

c.1532
Claude Garamont
[Garamond]

Some typefaces are relatively easy to describe, with a single designer and a date. We will meet more of these later in this book. However, a whole host of different typefaces bear the (slightly modified) name of the famous French punchcutter Claude Garamont and there is no space here to analyse their wayward family tree.

There's a typeface called Garamond, which was thought to be based on the work of Claude Garamont (1480–1561), but was revealed in the 1920s to be based instead on the (later) work of Jean Jannon (1580–1658). So the family tree is divided into Garamonds derived from Garamont's actual designs (themselves based on designs by Aldus Manutius, see page 12) and Garamonds based on Jannon.

The former includes Stempel Garamond (1924), Sabon (1967; see page 80) and Adobe Garamond, redrawn by Robert Slimbach, which was highly popular when issued in digital form in 1989. The Stempel Garamond is the only typeface in which both italic and roman are based on Garamont's originals.

The Jannon branch of the tree includes ATF Garamond drawn by Maurice Benton – later copied and ultimately digitized as Garamond 3; the Simoncini Garamond; and ITC Garamond (designed by Tony Stan, 1975), used by Pentagram's David Hillman for the italic 'The' in his 1987 redesign of *The Guardian*.

Specimen of Garamond from an undated booklet published by the D. Stempel foundry, c.1970s.

abcdefghijk12
LMNO,.£%*

Die stilechte Formung,

die außerordentliche Schönheit,

die vorzügliche Lesbarkeit

unserer

GARAMOND

kommen jedem Druck zustatten. Das Buch, die Zeitschrift,

der Industriekatalog, Anzeigen und Werbedrucke, Geschäfts-

und Familiendrucksachen erhalten durch die Garamond den

gewinnenden Ausdruck gepflegter typographischer Kultur.

GARAMOND *für schöne Drucke!*

GRANJON'S DOUBLE PICA ROMAN & ITALIC

1570–71
Robert Granjon

'The type designer's type designer'

The French punchcutter Robert Granjon (1513–89), active in
Paris and then Lyons in the middle of the sixteenth century, is
considered to be one of the greatest designers of italic types.
'Granjon is the type designer's type designer,' says Paul Barnes,
who believes that, of the Renaissance typefaces, the Double Pica
Roman & Italic is the one with 'the right balance between straight
lines and curves' – 'it is', he concludes, 'full of tension and beauty'.

Though there is a typeface called Granjon, this is actually
based on Garamond's designs (see page 14). The contemporary
typeface that revives Granjon's qualities is Matthew Carter's highly
versatile type family Galliard, released in several versions since
1978. Galliard's exuberant, authoritative curves can be seen in
academic books, journals and art catalogues worldwide. Its
distinctive italic characters, such as the lowercase 'g' and the
flamboyant uppercase 'Q' conjure Granjon's work with great flair.

Granjon is also remembered for his 'Civilité' style of type
(1557), which reflected the elegance of French handwriting,
including many *fleurons* (or typographic flowers) used for
decorations. Granjon intended this to become a national type
for France, but it fell out of favour after the sixteenth century,
and has not been revived, except as a curiosity.

Right: Typefaces cut
by Robert Granjon
(Ascendonica Romaine
and Ascendonica Cursive)
as printed in the Folio
Specimen (c.1585) of
the great Renaissance
printer-publisher Plantin.
Below left: An example of
'Galliard Roman' courtesy
of Matthew Carter.

Alfonsus rex Arrag. Idem dicere solet, ita demùm matrimonium tranquillè citráque querimonias exigi posse, si maritus surdus fiat, vxor cæca: innuens, opinor, fœmineum genus obnoxium esse zelotypiæ, atque hinc oriri rixas & querimonias: rursum maritis permolestam esse vxorum garrulitatē : qua molestia cariturus sit, si fiat surdus: nec illa vexabitur adulterıj suspicione, si careat oculis.

Valeria Messalarum soror, rogata, cur amisso Seruio viro, nulli vellet nubere : Quoniam, inquit, mihi semper viuit maritus Seruius.

ROMAIN DU ROI
Type design by committee

The Romain du Roi introduced a new kind of shape to type – the axes of its roman letters are vertical rather than angled (in the manner of handwriting). The new designs came about because Cardinal Richelieu, who had his own press, had urged King Louis XIII of France to found the Imprimerie royale in the Louvre Palace in Paris. In 1692 Louis XIV ordered a new series of types for the Imprimerie's own use, and the project was steered by the Académie des sciences, which appointed a committee to conduct extensive research.

Examples of the Romain du Roi designs can appear oddly digital, since the letterform designs are laid out against grid paper. Their design was a kind of 'sampling'. The Académie's committee examined exemplary handwriting styles – they considered handwritten books to be superior to printed ones – and produced an idealized form for each letter. (The types, with their finer lines and greater contrast reflected the handwriting of that era, which had moved on from the broken scripts and the broad-edge pen hands of earlier times.) The royal typecutter Philippe Grandjean (1666–1714) engraved the punches, though the project outlived him: the complete series of 82 fonts, both roman and italic, was not completed until 1745.

The Romain du Roi lower-case fonts include a small spur that sticks out of the middle of the left-hand side of the letter 'l' – an odd quirk that 'brands' the typeface as royal. They also included serifs on both sides of certain letters, and capital serifs that were finer than was customary, anticipating developments that would become crucial to later French typefaces such as Didot and Bodoni.

Examples of capital letters from the Romain du Roi, courtesy of Atelier du Livre d'art et de l'Estampe – Imprimerie nationale. The types are not an exact match to the engravings.

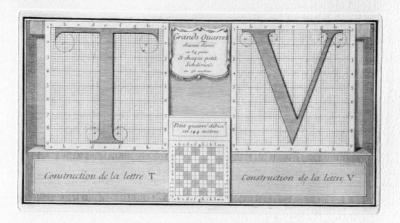

Construction de la lettre T

Construction de la lettre V

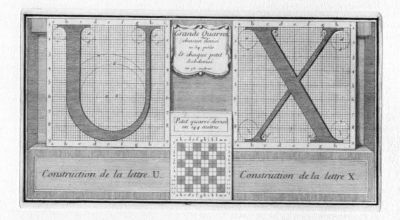

Construction de la lettre U

Construction de la lettre X

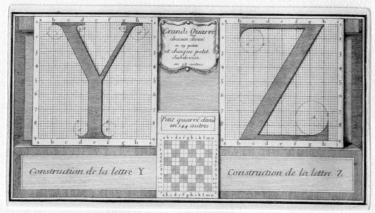

Construction de la lettre Y

Construction de la lettre Z

HC 1/10

CASLON
'When in doubt, set it in Caslon'

1725
William Caslon

The English baroque is epitomized by William Caslon (1692–1766), whose well-archived work has inspired dozens of copies bearing his name. Eric Gill described Caslon's letters as being 'at the same time good and ordinary … Caslon's Old Face is thoroughly decent in every respect.' The old printers' adage, 'When in doubt, set it in Caslon,' reflects the reassuring consistency of the 'brand name' – Frederick Goudy made a version (Caslon Old Face) in 1923; in 1989 Carol Twombly made a digital version (Adobe Caslon); and in 1994 Matthew Carter designed a version for use in display settings (Big Caslon).

William Caslon began as an engraver, but was asked to cut some Arabic types for some religious publications at a time (the 1720s) when there were few letter founders (as he called himself) in Britain. Perhaps sensing a gap in the market, he established a company to cut punches and produced an impressively comprehensive broadside specimen of his work in 1734. This widely reproduced document shows a broad variety of type in addition to the usual roman and italic, including black letter, Hebrew, Arabic, Armenian and 'Coptick'. (You can see Caslon's original punches at the St Bride Library near Fleet Street in London.)

A decade after Caslon's death, his types were used for the American Declaration of Independence.

abcdefghijk1
LMNO,.£%*

In CONGRESS, July 4, 1776.

A DECLARATION

By the REPRESENTATIVES of the

UNITED STATES OF AMERICA,

In GENERAL CONGRESS ASSEMBLED.

WHEN in the Course of human Events, it becomes neceſſary for one People to diſſolve the Political Bands which have connected them with another, and to aſſume among the Powers of the Earth, the ſeparate and equal Station to which the Laws of Nature and of Nature's God entitle them, a decent Reſpect to the Opinions of Mankind requires that they ſhould declare the cauſes which impel them to the Separation.

We hold theſe Truths to be ſelf-evident, that all Men are created equal, that they are endowed by their Creator with certain unalienable Rights, that among theſe are Life, Liberty, and the Purſuit of Happineſs—That to ſecure theſe Rights, Governments are inſtituted among Men, deriving their juſt Powers from the Conſent of the Governed, that whenever any Form of Government becomes deſtructive of theſe Ends, it is the Right of the People to alter or to aboliſh it, and to inſtitute new Government, laying its Foundation on ſuch Principles, and organizing its Powers in ſuch Form, as to them ſhall ſeem moſt likely to effect their Safety and Happineſs. Prudence, indeed, will dictate that Governments long eſtabliſhed ſhould not be changed for light and tranſient Cauſes; and accordingly all Experience hath ſhewn, that Mankind are more diſpoſed to ſuffer, while Evils are ſufferable, than to right themſelves by aboliſhing the Forms to which they are accuſtomed. But when a long Train of Abuſes and Uſurpations, purſuing invariably the ſame Object, evinces a Deſign to reduce them under abſolute Deſpotiſm, it is their Right, it is their Duty, to throw off ſuch Government, and to provide new Guards for their future Security. Such has been the patient Sufferance of theſe Colonies; and ſuch is now the Neceſſity which conſtrains them to alter their former Syſtems of Government. The Hiſtory of the preſent King of Great-Britain is a Hiſtory of repeated Injuries and Uſurpations, all having in direct Object the Eſtabliſhment of an abſolute Tyranny over theſe States. To prove this, let Facts be ſubmitted to a candid World.

He has refuſed his Aſſent to Laws, the moſt wholeſome and neceſſary for the public Good.

He has forbidden his Governors to paſs Laws of immediate and preſſing Importance, unleſs ſuſpended in their Operation till his Aſſent ſhould be obtained; and when ſo ſuſpended, he has utterly neglected to attend to them.

He has refuſed to paſs other Laws for the Accommodation of large Diſtricts of People, unleſs thoſe People would relinquiſh the Right of Repreſentation in the Legiſlature, a Right ineſtimable to them, and formidable to Tyrants only.

He has called together Legiſlative Bodies at Places unuſual, uncomfortable, and diſtant from the Depoſitory of their public Records, for the ſole Purpoſe of fatiguing them into Compliance with his Meaſures.

He has diſſolved Repreſentative Houſes repeatedly, for oppoſing with manly Firmneſs his Invaſions on the Rights of the People.

He has refuſed for a long Time, after ſuch Diſſolutions, to cauſe others to be elected; whereby the Legiſlative Powers, incapable of Annihilation, have returned to the People at large for their exerciſe; the State remaining in the mean time expoſed to all the Dangers of Invaſion from without, and Convulſions within.

He has endeavoured to prevent the Population of theſe States; for that Purpoſe obſtructing the Laws for Naturalization of Foreigners; refuſing to paſs others to encourage their Migrations hither, and raiſing the Conditions of new Appropriations of Lands.

He has obſtructed the Adminiſtration of Juſtice, by refuſing his Aſſent to Laws for eſtabliſhing Judiciary Powers.

He has made Judges dependent on his Will alone, for the Tenure of their Offices, and the Amount and Payment of their Salaries.

He has erected a Multitude of new Offices, and ſent hither Swarms of Officers to harraſs our People, and eat out their Subſtance.

He has kept among us, in Times of Peace, Standing Armies, without the conſent of our Legiſlatures.

He has affected to render the Military independent of and ſuperior to the Civil Power.

He has combined with others to ſubject us to a Juriſdiction foreign to our Conſtitution, and unacknowledged by our Laws; giving his Aſſent to their Acts of pretended Legiſlation:

For quartering large Bodies of Armed Troops among us:

For protecting them, by a mock Trial, from Puniſhment for any Murders which they ſhould commit on the Inhabitants of theſe States:

For cutting off our Trade with all Parts of the World:

For impoſing Taxes on us without our Conſent:

For depriving us, in many Caſes, of the Benefits of Trial by Jury:

For tranſporting us beyond Seas to be tried for pretended Offences:

For aboliſhing the free Syſtem of Engliſh Laws in a neighbouring Province, eſtabliſhing therein an arbitrary Government, and enlarging its Boundaries, ſo as to render it at once an Example and fit Inſtrument for introducing the ſame abſolute Rule into theſe Colonies:

For taking away our Charters, aboliſhing our moſt valuable Laws, and altering fundamentally the Forms of our Governments:

For ſuſpending our own Legiſlatures, and declaring themſelves inveſted with Power to legiſlate for us in all Caſes whatſoever.

He has abdicated Government here, by declaring us out of his Protection and waging War againſt us.

He has plundered our Seas, ravaged our Coaſts, burnt our Towns, and deſtroyed the Lives of our People.

He is, at this Time, tranſporting large Armies of foreign Mercenaries to compleat the Works of Death, Deſolation, and Tyranny, already begun with circumſtances of Cruelty and Perfidy, ſcarcely paralleled in the moſt barbarous Ages, and totally unworthy the Head of a civilized Nation.

He has conſtrained our fellow Citizens taken Captive on the high Seas to bear Arms againſt their Country, to become the Executioners of their Friends and Brethren, or to fall themſelves by their Hands.

He has excited domeſtic Inſurrections amongſt us, and has endeavoured to bring on the Inhabitants of our Frontiers, the mercileſs Indian Savages, whoſe known Rule of Warfare, is an undiſtinguiſhed Deſtruction, of all Ages, Sexes and Conditions.

In every ſtage of theſe Oppreſſions we have Petitioned for Redreſs in the moſt humble Terms: Our repeated Petitions have been anſwered only by repeated Injury. A Prince, whoſe Character is thus marked by every act which may define a Tyrant, is unfit to be the Ruler of a free People.

Nor have we been wanting in Attentions to our Britiſh Brethren. We have warned them from Time to Time of Attempts by their Legiſlature to extend an unwarrantable Juriſdiction over us. We have reminded them of the Circumſtances of our Emigration and Settlement here. We have appealed to their native Juſtice and Magnanimity, and we have conjured them by the Ties of our common Kindred to diſavow theſe Uſurpations, which, would inevitably interrupt our Connections and Correſpondence. They too have been deaf to the Voice of Juſtice and of Conſanguinity. We muſt, therefore, acquieſce in the Neceſſity, which denounces our Separation, and hold them, as we hold the reſt of Mankind, Enemies in War, in Peace, Friends.

We, therefore, the Repreſentatives of the UNITED STATES OF AMERICA, in General Congress, Aſſembled, appealing to the Supreme Judge of the World for the Rectitude of our Intentions, do, in the Name, and by Authority of the good People of theſe Colonies, ſolemnly Publiſh and Declare, That theſe United Colonies are, and of Right ought to be, Free and Independent States; that they are abſolved from all Allegiance to the Britiſh Crown, and that all political Connection between them and the State of Great-Britain, is and ought to be totally diſſolved; and that as Free and Independent States, they have full Power to levy War, conclude Peace, contract Alliances, eſtabliſh Commerce, and to do all other Acts and Things which Independent States may of right do. And for the ſupport of this Declaration, with a firm Reliance on the Protection of divine Providence, we mutually pledge to each other our Lives, our Fortunes, and our ſacred Honor.

Signed by ORDER and in BEHALF of the CONGRESS,

JOHN HANCOCK, President.

ATTEST.
CHARLES THOMSON, Secretary.

PHILADELPHIA: Printed by John Dunlap.

BASKERVILLE
Ahead of his time

1757
John Baskerville

The Birmingham printer John Baskerville (1706–75) was an inventor, an industrialist and an independent all-rounder, who went to great lengths to improve the technology of his day to make better-crafted, more readable books. As a printer, he was a late starter, working with his punchcutter, John Handy, to achieve 'greater accuracy' in 'the true proportion' of letterforms.

His exquisite 1757 Bible received hostile criticism at the time for its 'illegibility': readers were unused to the finer serifs made possible by his innovations in paper quality (the first wove surface), ink and finishing. Baskerville's perfectionism made him a controversial figure in Britain. His beautifully made books received more acclaim on the Continent than at home, and he failed to achieve commercial success as a printer.

Baskerville made several attempts to sell his printing equipment before his death, and in 1779 his widow sold the original punches to the French dramatist Beaumarchais (who wanted to print an edition of Voltaire). The punches eventually found their way to the French foundry Deberny & Peignot, who generously returned them to English soil in 1953.

Baskerville's nonconformist personality lives on in myriad versions of his famous typeface, which was revived to great success in the 1920s and has remained popular with designers and advertisers ever since.

Right: Title page from the 1763 Baskerville Bible, showing Baskerville's roman and italic faces in addition to elaborate blackletter titles.
Below: Designed in 2001, John McConnell's logo for the Japan Festival consists of a lower-case Baskerville 'j' with a red dot – in McConnell's own words, it's a 'classic bit of type and the Japanese flag'.

abcdefghi123
JKLM,.£%*

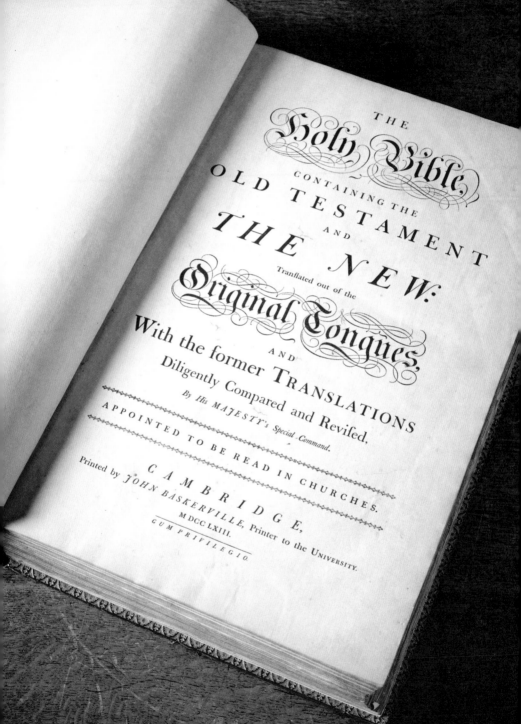

THE

Holy Bible

CONTAINING THE

OLD TESTAMENT

AND

THE NEW:

Translated out of the

Original Tongues,

AND

With the former TRANSLATIONS

Diligently Compared and Revised,

By His MAJESTY's Special Command.

APPOINTED TO BE READ IN CHURCHES.

CAMBRIDGE,

Printed by JOHN BASKERVILLE, Printer to the UNIVERSITY.

MDCCLXIII.

CUM PRIVILEGIO.

The typeface we now call Didot emerged in 1784, designed by Firmin Didot (1764–1836), the 19-year-old son of Françoise-Ambroise Didot, who had established the Didot system of measuring type. Both were members of a printing and publishing dynasty that spanned several generations. This graceful typeface, with fine serifs and a dramatic contrast between the thick and thin strokes, established a new look for letters, known as Moderns, that seemed a long way from type's origins in the handwriting of scribes.

Change was in the air – the typeface made its appearance just five years before the French Revolution – and the books that were printed with this new typeface reflected a fresh mood in politics and culture – less ornamented, possibly more democratic. Didot also benefited from improvements in printing and paper – the Didots, unlike Baskerville (see page 22), prospered from their innovations.

The typeface went out of favour late in the nineteenth century, but in the early twentieth century the French foundry Deberny & Peignot bought the original Didot punches and the typeface soon found favour with a new kind of designer – the 'magazine art director'. One such person was the influential Alexey Brodovitch, who art-directed *Harper's Bazaar* from 1934 to 1958. ('Didot was the black blade that cut the white space of [Brodovitch's] layouts,' observed the graphic designer Abbott Miller.)

In the early 1990s an important element of *Harper's Bazaar*'s famously radical redesign was a new, digital version of Didot, redrawn to exacting new standards by Jonathan Hoefler of Hoefler & Frere-Jones.

'Z' Type specimen of the new version of Didot that Jonathan Hoefler and Tobias Frere-Jones designed for *Harper's Bazaar* in 1991. The grand new family (of 42 fonts) emphasized the tension between thick strokes and X-ray hairlines in a way that could hardly be imagined in Firmin's day.

abcdefghijk12
LMNO,.£%*

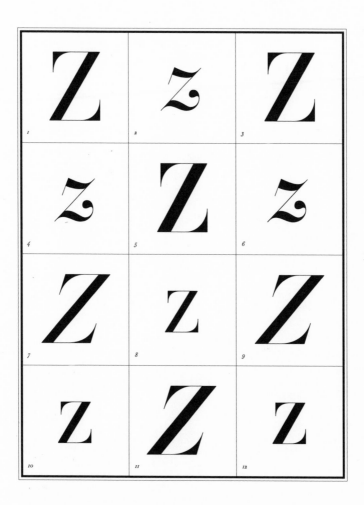

BODONI
Through thick and thin

late 1780s
Giambattista Bodoni

The typeface we call Bodoni, issued by several different foundries over the past century, takes its shape from the work of the prolific and precocious Italian printer and designer Giambattista Bodoni (1740–1813) of Parma. Like Didot and Walbaum (see pages 24 and 28), it is regarded as a 'modern', a class of typeface distinguished by contrasts between thick and thin strokes. These characteristics have come to be associated with elegance and luxury, which puts such fonts high on the list when designers tackle perfume packaging or fashion magazines such as *Vogue* or *W*.

By all accounts, Bodoni had a thorough grasp of all aspects of the publishing process – from letterform to finished book – and wrote extensively, publishing the *Epithalamia exoticis linguis reddita* (1775), which demonstrated 25 Asian and African languages. His designs reflect his observation that a typeface could be made from a small number of modular components. In the preface to the posthumously published *Manuale Tipografico* (1818), he states: 'It is proper here to offer the four different heads under which [...] are derived the beauties of type, and the first of these is regularity – conformity without ambiguity, variety without dissonance, and equality and symmetry without confusion.'

There are now more than 500 typefaces bearing the name 'Bodoni', so it is best to regard it as a sprawling family, with everything from rich relations to black sheep.

Kinetic sign ('Palindrome') by designers Troika for London's Victoria and Albert Museum, 2010. Three independently revolving elements are in constant motion, deconstructing and rebuilding the famous V&A logo designed by Pentagram's Alan Fletcher (1989), adapted from three characters of the Bodoni typeface.

abcdefgh123
IJKL,.£.?$&

WALBAUM
From jobbing type to book art

Justus Erich Walbaum

Walbaum is one of the Moderns, first cut in the early years of the nineteenth century by German typecutter Justus Erich Walbaum (1768–1839), and possibly inspired by Bodoni and Didot (see pages 26 and 24). Within German type history the design is regarded as an important break with the black-letter tradition.

Though it lacks the fashionable associations of Didot and Bodoni, Walbaum has nonetheless had an interesting afterlife: it is thought to be the model for the shape of Akzidenz Grotesk – the nineteenth-century 'jobbing type' that would eventually give rise to many of the sans-serif typefaces, such as Helvetica, that became so prominent in the twentieth century.

Walbaum had a chance encounter with the twentieth-century world of book art when when artist/polymath Tom Phillips embarked upon his monumental version of Dante's *Inferno* (Talfourd Press, 1983). For this limited edition, Phillips used a wide variety of print media, including silkscreen, lithography, etching and letterpress pages made with typographer Ian Mortimer.

Mortimer suggested that Phillips use the Walbaum typeface because of its similarity to the jobbing type (an 'English Modern') used in W. H. Mallock's *A Human Document*, a Victorian novel that Phillips had extensively reworked into the poetic and highly acclaimed *A Humument* (1973–). The Dante pages also use words taken from the Mallock via *A Humument*, which Phillips reworks to this day. Later versions of Walbaum were designed by Gunter Gerhard Lange (H. Berthold AG, 1976) and Frantisek Storm (2010).

A page from the 1983 edition of Tom Phillips's Dante, using the typeface Walbaum, printed by Ian Mortimer at his private press I. M. Imprimit. The typeface achieved other cultural associations through the type-only Penguin editions of Graham Greene's novels designed by Derek Birdsall in the early 1970s.

abcdefg123
LMN,.£%*"

But now the time has come. Stretch out your hand;
unseal my eyes.' I did not open them.
To treat him ill was courtesy enough.
You Genoese! You're strangers all of you
to every decency of life; you're full
of everything corrupt. I don't know why
you have not yet been banished from the earth!
For with Romagna's most repugnant soul
I found one son of yours who for his works
bathes in Cocytus even now, in soul,
yet still, in body, seems to walk the world.

THE FIRST 'FAT FACE'
A blast of vulgarity

1803
Robert Thorne
for Thorowgood

The London type founder Robert Thorne (1754–1820) is thought to have designed the first 'fat-face' typeface to meet the demand for more arresting type for posters and broadsheets – a sudden and refreshing blast of vulgarity in the first decades of the nineteenth century. This also marked a change in the way type foundries sold their wares – from books to advertising.

The posters needed to promote the popular lotteries of the time encouraged the production of loud fat faces – that is, until 1824, when the government stamped down on gambling. (Curiously, William Thorowgood went on to buy Thorne's foundry with the proceeds of a successful lottery win.)

Fat faces were also frequently used for the title pages of popular pamphlets, as well as display lines in broadsides, ballads and news pamphlets that recounted sensational happenings, murders, deaths by fire, and so on. 'The last dying words of some murderer … generally had a heading set in a Fat Face,' wrote A F Johnson in the British typography periodical *Alphabet & Image* no. 5 (1947).

Right: In 1986, Ed Fella designed a postmodern tribute to Thorne's distinctive typeface. Fella is a former sign-writer who had gone to the Cranbrook Academy of Art, near Detroit – then a hotbed of radical typography – as a mature student.
Below: Detail of specimen page from Thorowgood's *New Specimen of Printing Types*, 1821.

FIVE LINE PICA No. 5.

R. THORNE
Blackburn
Manchester
£2345678

AGGRAVATE

Ample Notice Is Given As The Precious Becomes Girth

a **Robert Thorne**, no doubt *a portly* gent, thin limbed and top hatted, cheeky **&** dark, *born unknown*, a foundling for sure, finds only a euphony of *eye* where a *body* of exuberance is needed. Stretching, *he* DOUBLED, then drew the *very first fat face* letterforms in the *Great Britain* of 1803. Turning to the **bold of the Industrial Revolution** *(1760————1840)*, he fills out the **demand for bloat.**

As power **SHIFTS** *in a great* *hundredfold* **INCREASE** *steaming:* throbbing, cranking, hurling quavering **&** *in flux:*

into this age for the *expansive,* that rise of the vast: DREAD along with *the cheap and the quick.* **And** NOW *observe* the newly corpulent in a *role* of substance *pad* the ephemera of **PRINTED VERBOSITY** *from out of the tiny title page text* faces to the scale *change* of building side DISPLAY *faces,* posted in a great **SHOW** of *mingled garrulity.*

Type Poster: Cranbrook Graduate Design Student Project | Graphic Design | Illustration | Seasons Greetings | Edward Fella 1986

THE FIRST EGYPTIANS (SLAB SERIFS)

As English as warm beer

1810
and after...
Vincent Figgins,
Robert Thorne,
William Thorowgood,
Robert Besley...

The word 'Egyptian' is another of those misleading terms that can confuse the unwary – naming slab serifs this way has nothing to do with Egypt; it was just a fashionable nickname at the time when typefaces with squared-off serifs came into widespread use.

The invention of steam-powered presses during the second decade of the nineteenth century helped boost the growth of advertising posters. These required typefaces that shouted their wares to the public, and the new wave of Egyptians did the trick. Fast-forward nearly two centuries, and slab serifs are again in the spotlight, seen everywhere from UK daily *The Guardian* to electronic devices such as the Kindle.

The first slab-serif type was the Antique of Vincent Figgins (1766–1844), first published in 1817 in four sizes, but in capitals only. The ailing Robert Thorne (see page 30) made an Egyptian in several sizes, published posthumously by William Thorowgood, his successor, in 1821. Thorowgood was a novice who used his fortune to set up as 'Letter-Founder to his majesty'.

The slab serif typeface named Clarendon was issued by Thorowgood's Fann Street Foundry in 1845, its design credited to Robert Besley (1794–1876). Though Clarendon was the first typeface to be copyrighted, it was a great commercial success and consequently soon copied and pirated. Like 'Egyptian', the term 'Clarendon' is often used as a generic term for a slab serif.

After half a century of success, slab serifs fell out of favour – to be revived in the 1930s and then in the 1950s, when the Sheffield foundry Stephenson Blake went back to the Fann Street originals to produce Consort. Hermann Eidenbenz (1902–93) designed a new version (1950) for Stempel.

The Design Research Unit (DRU) identity for the Watneys chain of pubs in the 1960s made use of a sloping Clarendon. A staple of mid-twentieth-century UK sign-making that serves the needs of trendies and traditionalists alike, the sturdy Clarendon, erect or sloping, seems as British as warm beer. Photo: John Maltby.

abcdefg12
IJKL,.£%*

THE FIRST SANS SERIFS
Barbaric strength in capital letters

Though it occupies a special place in type history books, the first upper-case sans serif (confusingly named Egyptian; see page 30) was not really (as far as we know) used very much at all. The man behind it, William Caslon IV, was the grandson of the first William Caslon.

By the 1830s, when William Thorowgood produced his Seven-line Grotesque – the first sans serif with a lower case – this more 'realist' form of type caught a darker, more earnest mood within popular culture. Historian Nicolete Gray described the development in her *Nineteenth Century Ornamented Typefaces*: 'flowing italics and jovial lower case letters are out of favour. In their place are compressed fat faces and heavy sans serifs.' By the mid-nineteenth century, type founders throughout the Western world were producing every kind of sans serif in every width and weight – sans-serif type was here to stay.

In a celebrated essay (now a short book) entitled 'The Nymph and the Grot', James Mosley traces the possible sources of the sans-serif (or grotesque) form, taking in Imperial Roman letters, a Greek inscription in marble, maps, buildings and a 1748 inscription in a grotto in Stourhead, Wiltshire. Mosley concluded that the sans serif's appeal lay in its barbaric strength and absence of ornament. He notes that it might have remained a curiosity if the 'English sign-writers and type founders had not exploited it for their own purposes with an almost complete disregard for classical propriety, and thus preserved it for its later career.'

Right: Detail from the 1819 edition of the Blake, Garnett & Co type specimen, which includes a page featuring 'W Caslon Junr Letterfounder'. Right below: Detail from the 1834 type specimen of William Thorowgood.

CUMBERLAND.

TYPOGRAPHY.

W CASLON JUNR   LETTERFOUNDER

SALISBURY SQUARE.

MENINCHURNE

mountainous

THOROWGOOD, LONDON.

POUCHÉE DECORATIVE ALPHABETS
A decorative rediscovery

c.1823
Louis John [Jean] Pouchée

These beautiful decorative boxwood display types were largely ignored, shipped from archive to archive until the 1960s, when they ended up in safe hands at St Bride Library off Fleet Street, in London. These artifacts are not actual pieces of type, but patterns that made metal moulds (some of which also survive) that in turn would make type.

Louis John Pouchée (1782–1845) was not well known in his time. His foundry paid high wages but charged low prices for type, making him doubly unpopular with his rivals. His type foundry closed in 1830 after just 12 years in operation, and his materials were sold by auction.

When St Bride librarian James Mosley and artist Ian Mortimer made some prints from the blocks in the 1980s, their intricate beauty was a revelation. The basic, seriffed shapes of the letters are embellished with elaborate illustrative and decorative elements. An agricultural alphabet includes animals, labourers and farming implements. Others include autumn fruits, flowers and vines, while a Masonic alphabet includes symbols such as compasses and candlesticks.

Since Ian Mortimer and Julia Horsfall published a limited edition of these alphabets in 1993 (*Ornamented Types: Twenty-three Alphabets from the Foundry of Louis John Pouchée*), some of Pouchée's designs have emerged in commercial use, including in the cover artwork for the Pulp album *We Love Life* (2001) and a Phaidon gardening book.

Right: The second of two index pages from *Ornamented Types: Twenty-Three alphabets from the foundry of Louis John Pouchée* published by I. M. Imprimit (Ian Mortimer) in association with the St. Bride Printing Library, 1992.
Below: An original wood engraving used as a pattern for Pouchée's 17-Line No. 1 decorated alphabet, 1820s.

14 Lines No. 3
Lacks P; G STOCK are stereos
2 sheets

16 Lines No. 2
3 sheets

16 Lines No. 1
3 sheets

17 Lines
There are two forms of N
3 sheets

18 Lines No. 1
3 sheets

18 Lines No. 2
3 sheets

26 Lines
5 sheets

ADDITIONAL ALPHABETS

[14-line pica]
4 sheets

12 Lines Pica Ornamented
M is a modern line-plate

WOOD TYPES – CONDENSED GROTESQUES

How wood type won the West

The first-known wood-type catalogue appeared in 1828, soon after New York printer Darius Wells (1800–75) developed a lateral router, with which wood letters could be mass-produced. Because wood letters were much lighter than metal, this was a great advance for printers who specialized in posters.

You can see the immediate effect of this development in American theatre and circus posters in the mid-nineteenth century. In the Wild West, the new wood type heralded an explosion of every kind of display type, from rugged Antiques and Clarendons (see page 32) to the most fantastical and elaborately ornamented faces. The new techniques eventually spread to Europe during the Victorian era.

By 1840 Wells, who had started out in the 1820s cutting wood type by hand, wrote confidently that 'The manufacture of Wood Type formed a new era in job printing … In regard to their cheapness and durability, no argument is now necessary.'

The wood-type business went into permanent decline by the start of the twentieth century, but the designs live on: in everything from Victoriana (such as the circus poster referenced in the Beatles song 'Being for the Benefit of Mr Kite') to the 'Entertaining types' repurposed by Alan Kitching (1940–) and Celia Stothard (1949–2010).

Right: Alan Kitching's wood type cover for a 150th anniversary book about the Albert Hall, 2003. The design practice Untitled approached Kitching after looking at archive photos of the Albert Hall, which featured posters using large wood-letter poster type in capitals only. Kitching used the curve of the Hall's oval shape to make the type hang together like a carnival banner.
Below: detail from page 116 of *American Wood Type 1828–1900* by Rob Roy Kelly (Van Nostrand Reinhold Company, 1969). Copyright Reinhold Book Corporation.

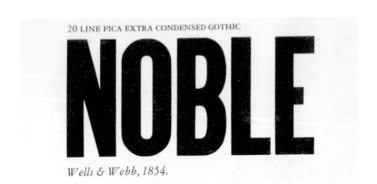

20 LINE PICA EXTRA CONDENSED GOTHIC

NOBLE

Wells & Webb, 1854.

THE ROYAL ALBERTHALL

THE FIRST TYPEWRITER 1868
Victorian desktop publishing

In 1868, after a few false starts, Henry Latham Scholes patented the typewriter, which at first had only capitals. Typewriter design had little connection with the type industry, but the IBM Selectric 'golfball' typewriter (1961) made possible an early form of what would later be called 'desktop publishing'. The machine produced decent-looking columns of text that that could be pasted up as part of the 'camera-ready' artwork for an independent magazine publisher, and typefaces could be changed by switching the 'golfball'.

The 'default' look of type made by a typewriter – monospaced and with variations in evenness that depended upon the typist's skill – has prompted several type designs, of which Joel Kaden and Tony Stan's American Typewriter (1974) is perhaps the best known. Other typewriter fonts include Courier (designed by Howard Kettler in 1955), one of the first fonts available to the early laser printers; Trixie (LettError, 1991), which deliberately mimicked the blotchy letters of a badly maintained portable; and A2 Typewriter (2010), Henrik Kubel's elegant rethink of the genre.

For Pentagram's Michael Bierut, 'the classic, frozen-in-amber application of American Typewriter remains the three black capital letters that surround the red heart in Milton Glaser's "I Love New York" logo. Any attempt to rip it off doesn't quite work unless it's set in American Typewriter.'

Milton Glaser's 'I Love New York' logo (1975) in action: on Banksy's giant rat; modelled by comedian Tracy Morgan; stuck on a bumper; or capturing popular sentiment a week after the 2001 attacks on the World Trade Center. Glaser wanted the logo to be informal. 'It was somewhere between typography and a note,' he says. 'I wanted a counterpoint to the voluptuous and erotic nature of the heart.' Glaser asked his colleague George Leavitt to modify the letters of the American Typewriter typeface so that they would be less rounded.

abcdefg123
LMNO,.£%

STENCIL-GOTHIC / STENCIL
Give us a break

c.1885
John West for
MacKellar,
Smiths & Jordon

As a form of letter-making and printing, stencils predate the beginning of moveable type – whether you locate that in 1455 Mainz (Gutenberg's time) or eleventh-century China – by centuries.

The stencil mark is derived from cuts made in paper, card or metal. The letters with counters (the holes in 'a', 'b', 'o' and so on) contain 'breaks' that keep the stencil together, but interrupt the lines. Though some users modify the letters by inking in the gaps, it's the breaks that give stencils their archetypal 'look'.

It took time for type founders to imitate this in type. In the 1880s the Philadelphia foundry MacKellar, Smiths & Jordon produced Stencil-Gothic, a decorative typeface designed by John West that combined a thick stencil letter with decorative fronds and petals.

Yet there would be little typeface activity in this area until the 1920s, when the stencil-like Schablonenschrift (designed by Josef Albers) and Futura Black (Paul Renner) emerged. Le Corbusier used Didot-like French stencil letters (made by Thévenon & Cie) for his architectural publications.

In 1937 two foundries – Ludlow in the UK and ATF in the States – opened up the market for stencil type with two designs. Both were named Stencil. Soon after this came Tea Chest (Stephenson Blake, c.1939) and later there was Chaillot (Deberny & Peignot, 1951) and then all manner of stencil faces. In 2012 John Morgan Studio designed a bespoke stencil font, based on Venetian stencilled *nizioletti* (street-name) signs, for the Venice Architecture Biennale. Morgan's project – identity design for the Biennale – won the graphic design category of the Design Museum's Designs of the Year Awards in 2013.

Right: Stencil faces have been useful in communicating the horny-handed cultures of building sites, railfreight, shipping and also military life – as in this poster for Robert Altman's film *M*A*S*H* (1970). Below: detail of specimen for Stencil-Gothic, c.1885, a little-used typeface recently rediscovered by stencil expert Eric Kindel.

REFORMING POLITICIANS
EXTREMELY VISIONARY UNDERTAKING
1234567890

42

M*A*S*H
gives a
D*A*M*N

AKZIDENZ GROTESK (STANDARD)

1896–9
Berthold foundry

From jobbing type to Swiss Modernism

Akzidenz Grotesk is a nineteenth-century everyday typeface (*Akzidenzschrift* means 'jobbing type' in German) originally cut by largely anonymous, nineteenth-century punchcutters at the Berthold foundry and elsewhere. It was intended for display rather than running text, but its forms may have been modelled on Walbaum, the serif typeface then popular in Germany (see page 28).

For the Constructivists, the Bauhaus radicals and their successors, this workmanlike font matched the new search for *Sachlichkeit* (objectivity), and within a generation the typeface became a frequent and easily recognizable component of the New Typography that sprang from Switzerland in the post-war era. You can see it in striking advertisements, magazines, posters and book covers by Max Bill, Josef Müller-Brockmann, Max Huber, Carlo Vivarelli and many others. By the 1950s the popularity and utility of this grotesque, marketed by Berthold abroad as Standard, led to the development (by rival type foundries) of Univers and Helvetica (see pages 74 and 72).

Berthold's designer Günter Gerhard Lange (1921–2008) helped develop the typeface, through photosetting and into the digital era, into an extensive family. Akzidenz Grotesk has remained popular with designers such as Daniel Eatock (who uses little else) and Mike Joyce, whose witty Swissted website reimagines punk posters in a deliberately anachronistic pastiche of Swiss Modernism.

International style: 'New Forms in Italy', 1954, a poster by Swiss designer Carlo Vivarelli (1919–86) using Akzidenz Grotesk at two sizes on a flag-like grid. Vivarelli studied in Paris and worked in Milan before returning to Zurich in the 1940s. In 1958 he co-founded the influential *Neue Grafik* magazine, a great proponent of the new typography that was largely coming from Switzerland.

abcdefghij12
LMNO,.£%*"

Juni-Festwochen Zürich

Forme nuove in Italia

1954

Zürich

Kunstgewerbemuseum
Ausstellung
Forme nuove in Italia

Offen: 10-12, 14-18, Mittw. bis 21
Samstag/Sonntag bis 17
Montag geschlossen

Dauer: 12. Juni bis 31. Juli 1954

Entwurf C. L. Vivarelli · Druck: Bollmann AG

CHELTENHAM
The first font family

1896/1903
Bertram Grosvenor
Goodhue / Maurice
Fuller Benton for ATF

Cheltenham was one of the most popular typefaces of the twentieth century, and its traces can still be seen everywhere, from the opening titles for the BBC soap opera *EastEnders* to the headlines of the *New York Times* (for whom it was digitized by Matthew Carter) in both paper and app versions.

Originally designed in 1896 by architect Bertram Grosvenor Goodhue (1869–1924) as an easily readable book typeface for the New York-based Cheltenham Press, it was made commercially available by American Type Founders (ATF) in 1903, and quickly acquired a reputation not for books but for display – in advertisements, headlines and subheads, and so on. Over the following decade Maurice Fuller Benton (1872–1948), head of ATF's design department, made a set of variations that encouraged and met printers' demands for versatile display typefaces. Benton's 'Chelts' became effectively the first font family.

From the outset, Cheltenham was a popular success that drew controversy – much as Comic Sans and Helvetica prompt ferocious arguments in the present day. Douglas C McMurtrie, a much-admired typographic guru, wrote: 'The appearance of most magazine and commercial printing will be improved by the simple expedient of denying any variants of the Cheltenham design to compositors.' Even Daniel Berkeley Updike, who had helped introduce Goodhue to the Cheltenham Press, wrote: 'Owing to certain eccentricities of form, in cannot be read comfortably for any length of time. […] It is, however, an exceedingly handsome letter for ephemeral printing.'

Right: Page from an undated American Type Founders (ATF) brochure titled *The Cheltenham Wide*, c.1915. Below: cover of a undated ATF specimen book entitled *Cheltenham Old Style*, probably 1920s.

abcdefghij123
LMNO,.£%"

Cheltenham

Wide

Wide 72

Wide 60

Wide 48

Wide 42

Wide 36

Wide 30

Wide 24

Wide 18

Wide 14

Wide 12

Wide 11

Wide 10

Wide 8

Wide 6

Cheltenham

Italic 72

Italic 60

Italic 48

Italic 42

Italic 36

Italic 30

Italic 24

Italic 18

Italic 14

Italic 12

Italic 11

Italic 10

Italic 8

Italic 6

AMERICAN TYPE FOUNDERS CO.

RENAISSANCE ORNAMENT NO. 14

FRANKLIN GOTHIC CONDENSED

To see and be seen

1903–14
Morris Fuller Benton

The prolific type designer Morris Fuller Benton devised this heavy typeface at the beginning of the hot-metal revolution, and its success led him to develop it as a family. 'Gothics', the US name for those sturdy sans-serif typefaces that the Germans called 'Grotesks' and the English called Antiques, had been going strong for half a century or more, under a variety of names, widths and sizes. Such typefaces were once poetically described by Robert Bringhurst as 'cultural souvenirs of the bleakest days of the Industrial Revolution'.

Benton's stroke of genius was to consolidate these different forms under one, very American-sounding brand name that ATF could then promote and sell – with huge success. Franklin Gothic was even more of a hit in the United States than Cheltenham (another Benton-guided family; see page 46), and it has retained its credibility where other faces have disappeared from view.

Franklin Gothic Condensed has acquired another layer of meaning for anyone aware of contemporary conceptual art: it's the habitual choice for Lawrence Weiner's text-based pieces – grand but often ambiguous statements displayed in large capitals against a white wall or page, such as: 'Bits & pieces put together to present a semblance of a whole' (1991). 'Franklin Gothic did not represent me,' says Weiner, who also describes it as the 'working class typeface'. 'I preferred to be represented by it.'

'STEEL PENNIES THAT DID NOT COME FROM HEAVEN STREWN AT THE LEVEL OF THE SEA' (2008), an installation by Lawrence Weiner at Marian Goodman Gallery, New York. The first nine words of this artwork are in Franklin Gothic EF Extra Condensed.

abcdefghij12 LMNO,.£%*"

STEEL PENNIES
THAT DID NOT
COME FROM
HEAVEN

STREWN

AT THE LEVEL
OF THE SEA

JOHNSTON SANS
Ageless calm in the Underground

1918
Edward Johnston

The sans-serif typeface that the master calligrapher Edward Johnston (1872–44) drew for the London Underground continues to be one of the most effective and best-loved examples of typographic identity. Johnston was commissioned by Frank Pick, the enlightened commercial manager of what was then the London Electric Railway Company, to draw a new display typeface that would help rationalize the sprawling network of Underground lines. First known as Underground, it was later called Johnston Railway and then Johnston Sans (or simply Johnston).

Johnston, who also taught calligraphy, began work on designs for his typeface in 1915, and produced several versions over the next two decades. Typographic scholar Justin Howes explained its perennial appeal thus:

> It is clear. It works well at several sizes, and remains readable whether seen close-to or from afar. It is rather heavier than most sans-serif typefaces designed for print, but without being bold, and has a robustness necessary in designing a type used for signage.

Unlike the 'jobbing' grotesques of the nineteenth century, Johnston Sans was deliberately modelled on an ancient Roman antecedent – the letters around the base of Trajan's Column (completed 113 CE).

Johnston Sans, in partnership with the familiar circular logo (the 'Roundel', also designed by Johnston), lives on in today's network and in totally new services such as the Docklands Light Railway and the new Overground. Its influence is visible in the typeface Gill Sans (see page 60), now the public face of the BBC.

Right: Edward Johnston's design guidelines for the Underground 'Roundel', 1925. The drawing shows a fully lined-out 'standard' roundel, with the exact proportions and colours to be used together with the Underground lettering, 1925.
Right below: When the 2012 London Olympics chose for its logo what critic Jonathan Glancey called a 'symbol of pure chaos', with a typeface to match, Johnston Sans continued to look calm and ageless, guiding visitors through the capital with a minimum of fuss.

abcdefghijk12
LMNO,.£%*"

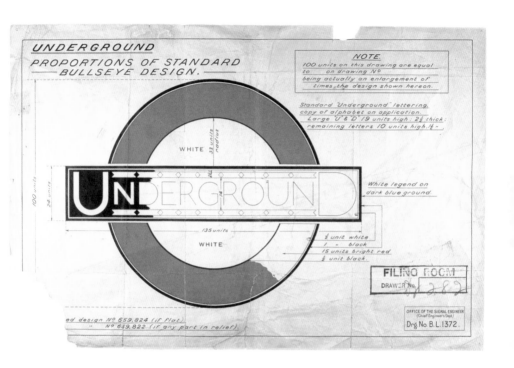

COOPER BLACK
Cooper's counters keep on truckin'

1921
Oswald B Cooper
for Barnhart Brothers
& Spindler

If any typeface could be said to wear a smile, it's Cooper Black, one of the most easily recognizable typefaces of the twentieth century. With its sexy, unthreatening curves and the jaunty rake of the space (technically a 'counter') in its 'o' and 'q', which leans back like the character in Robert Crumb's 'Keep on truckin'' cartoon, Cooper Black is a mainstay of snack bars, special offers and soft porn. Ward Nicolaas's celebration of Cooper Black, *BIG Black & Beautiful* (2011), compares the voluptuous typeface with the Venus of Willendorf and Marilyn Monroe.

Cooper Black was based on an earlier display face, also designed by Oswald B Cooper (1879–1940), called Cooper Old Style. Big and brash and manufactured in wood and metal for Barnhart Brothers & Spindler, it became a highly popular advertising face, in the United States, for which the foundry's own press ads targeted 'far-sighted printers with near-sighted customers'.

Despite its roots in 1920s hucksterism, Cooper Black is a jolie-laide typeface that seems to transcend fashion, attaching itself to all kinds of products and services, with or without irony as required: easyJet, Miles Davis, the Beach Boys' *Pet Sounds* album, *Dad's Army* and (with the addition of swashes) in 1970s 'adult' movies by Russ Meyer and Just Jaeckin. It's the face on a million T-shirts. The unapologetic and good-humoured vulgarity and utility of the typeface may ensure its longevity.

Clockwise from top left: Garfield and Odie, from Jim Davis's comic strip *Garfield*, on a US postage stamp, 2010; advertising poster for Levy's rye bread by Doyle Dane Bernbach, 1960; the familiar orange livery of easyJet, launched in 1995; a chalk-drawn café sign in Camberwell; the 1976 annual for the highly successful comedy series *Dad's Army*, which ran on BBC television from 1968 to 1977.

abcdef123
LM,.£% * "

You don't have to be Jewish

DAD'S ARMY

annual 1976

...ed edition based on the
... funny Television Series

CAFE OPEN

DIN 1451
Letters by and for engineers

1923–31
Anonymous engineers
for Stempel

The typeface known as DIN 1451 was made not by type designers but by German engineers as part of the Deutsche Industrienorm (DI-Norm – the 'German Industry Standard') established during the Weimar Republic. You can see versions of the typeface stamped on to German cars, tanks and aeroplane parts, and on the country's road signs. In recent years it has acquired a cult status, used by designers who value its 'undesigned' look for car advertisements and techno albums.

Yet for many years, despite its role as Germany's 'national typeface', DIN was something of an 'outsider' alphabet, often excluded from histories of type design. This is because its lines and curves are unsophisticated, with a continuous stroke width and a geometric look that parallels early Bauhaus alphabets and the much more sophisticated Futura (see page 58). DIN's letters can be drawn with rulers, compasses and stencils; they are intended for information rather than comfortable reading.

Albert-Jan Pool (1960–), who in 1994 designed the FF DIN, the typeface's versatile update, explains: 'The continuous stroke width is contradictory to the principles of traditional typography, where it is assumed that only varying stroke width will enable optimal word-images.' Pool's version is now a favourite with designers of magazines and cultural events and was used by the Swiss-French designer Ruedi Baur for the striking redesign (1997–2001) of the visual identity of the Centre Pompidou in Paris.

German road sign using the DIN typeface, photographed by Juergen Effner.

abcdefghij123
LMNO,.£%*"

Hamburg
Wedding

 Tegel

IONIC NO. 5 AND THE 'LEGIBILITY' GROUP OF TYPEFACES

News that's fit to read

1925–6
Chauncey H Griffith
for Linotype

In the earlier part of the twentieth century, newspapers played an essential role in the lives of millions. Yet, by the mid-1920s, the American press was in a moribund state as it confronted competition from the burgeoning new medium of radio. Spindly type and poor, high-speed printing had resulted in newspapers that were difficult to read.

Newspaper typefaces depended upon the fast-changing technology of hot-metal casters made by Linotype, Intertype and others. Linotype consolidated its powerful grip on the news industry by introducing its 'Legibility' group of typefaces under the direction of Chauncey H Griffith (1879–1956), who began by designing Ionic no. 5 in 1925.

Ionic was the first typeface designed to solve the problems posed by new technologies such as stereotyping and high-speed printing. Griffith was a former Linotype salesman from Kentucky who was promoted and had a long career as the company's design supremo. In March 1926 the *Newark Evening News* switched to Ionic no. 5. By the end of the following year, more than 3,000 newspapers around the world had followed suit by using Ionic as their text face. As Linotype sought to improve news type, it released more 'Legibility' typefaces such as Corona, Excelsior, Opticon, Paragon and Textype.

The printing facilities at the *Newark Evening News*, New Jersey, 1929.

abcdefg123 LMN,.£%*"

FUTURA
Geometry is never wrong

1927
Paul Renner for Bauer

Created by the German typographer Paul Renner (1878–1956), Futura is a sans typeface that seems redolent of its time and place (interwar Europe) yet still contemporary, adding its cool detachment to art catalogues, magazines and cult movies, like a hipster counterpart to the more British-seeming Gill Sans.

Futura's shapes were based on geometrical forms – ones that can be created by the triangle, the set square and the compass – rather than historical precedents. The ambition to reject traditional letterforms in favour of a more 'rational' approach was shared by Renner's near-contemporaries on the Weimar industrial standardization committee that published the DI-Norm (see page 54) and by Herbert Bayer, who completed a lowercase-only typeface called Universal while at the Bauhaus in 1925.

Renner's original designs included several experimental alternative characters that were omitted in the original releases for metal type by the Bauer foundry. Futura soon became a great success worldwide, and the foundry expanded the family to meet the demand for different weights and style.

In the 1990s Freda Sack and David Quay of The Foundry released a typeface they called Architype Renner, which included the letters missing from Bauer's version of Futura. These alternative shapes, such as a highly abstracted lower-case 'g' made from circle, triangle and two lines, evoke an innocent, 1920s vision of the future.

Despite its utopian beginnings, Futura has been used for all manner of ultra-corporate brands, including Mobil, Calvin Klein (right) and Volkswagen, whose tradition of distinctive advertising – beginning with Helmut Crone's memorable 1960s campaigns (below) – is aided by the typeface's subtle eccentricities.

abcdefghi12
LMNO,.£%"

You know what practice makes.

GILL SANS
The sans with a British accent?

1928
Eric Gill

Through a mix of design, inspired engineering, shrewd marketing and happenstance, the typeface by sculptor and stonecutter Eric Gill (1882–1940) has become the best-known British sans-serif typeface. Gill Sans gives consistent identity to items and institutions as different as the John Lewis department store chain, the Church of England's prayer book and the BBC.

Monotype's technicians guided Gill's original drawings through the careful production process necessary to make metal type for machine setting, and the typeface became a big hit. After some initial controversy within the business, Gill Sans was welcomed as a more human and no-nonsense response to the more geometric German sans serifs, and it was adopted by printers of every stripe. It has some similarities with Johnston Sans, as if Gill Sans were that typeface's more generalist, younger cousin.

The London and North Eastern Railway (LNER) used it for every aspect of its activities, from the nameplate of the *Flying Scotsman* locomotive through to menus, matchbooks and timetables. A triumphant blurb in *The Monotype Recorder* declared that the typeface came as a 'live destroyer of dead metal and dead categories – such as "artistic job", or "mere commercial printing"', and in that respect it anticipated the rise of the pragmatic independent graphic designers who emerged in the 1960s.

However, Gill Sans was not easily available in the United States, where typefaces such as Futura and Franklin Gothic held sway. The typeface's relative geographical isolation may have helped reinforce the notion that Gill Sans always speaks with a British accent.

Right: The cover of *Common Worship: Services and Prayers for the Church of England,* designed by Derek Birdsall and John Morgan, 2000
Right below: BBC logotype in Gill Sans capitals, known internally at the corporation as the 'BBC blocks'. Identity design by Martin Lambie-Nairn, 1997.
Below: Eric Gill's own type drawings for L.N.E.R. (London and North-Eastern Railway), dated 8 March 1933 and initialled by the designer.

abcdefghijk12
LMNO,.£%"

Common Worship

Services and Prayers for the Church of England

TIMES NEW ROMAN (AKA TIMES ROMAN)
Fit for purpose

1932
Stanley Morison
and Victor Lardent
for Monotype

In 1929 *The Times* newspaper invited Monotype's Stanley Morison (1889–1967) to submit ideas after he had published an article critical of the newspaper's design – in his view, *The Times*'s type was in a typographic cul-de-sac. The result was a complete revision of its text type, which became known as Times Roman. The new typeface was cut to be legible for every aspect of the paper's daily production, from the smallest listings to the headlines. Morison, who was not a draftsman, worked with Monotype's Victor Lardent (1905–68), asking him to study a sixteenth-century page printed by Antwerp printer Christopher Plantin, whose types were cut by Robert Granjon. (There is also a hotly debated theory, advanced by the type authority Mike Parker, that Times Roman was based on drawings by the boat-builder William Starling Burgess in 1904.)

The new sharply defined typeface soon found favour as a versatile and legible face for a wide range of journals and books when it became available to non-*Times* publications. (It was not widely copied by other newspapers because *The Times* used more expensive paper and printing than its rivals.) In 1946 the design critic Peggy Lang wrote: 'The final result of this enterprise was probably the most striking application of "fitness for purpose" to a contemporary typographical requirement … People with poor eyesight discovered that they could read the paper for the first time.'

After some time in the typographic wilderness, Times New Roman made an accidental comeback in the 1980s when it was one of just four typefaces (along with Helvetica, Courier and Zapf Dingbats) installed in the first Apple LaserWriter printers.

Times New Roman made its first appearance in print in the 3 October 1932 issue of *The Times* (below right). Thanks to its anonymous ubiquity, it might be the most-read typeface in the world, the first-choice font for 'lost pet' printouts on tree trunks and lampposts. Stanley Morison himself wrote: 'It has the merit of not looking as if it had been designed by somebody in particular.'

abcdefghij12
MNO,.£%*"

FAMILY CAT MISSING

THE TIMES

LONDON MONDAY OCTOBER 3 1932

ALBERTUS
The voice of authority

1932–40
Berthold Wolpe

This beguiling typeface, originally designed as a capitals-only display font, speaks in many tongues but it is frequently used as the voice of quiet, firm authority. It can be seen in the many Faber book jackets by the German-born designer Berthold Wolpe (1905–89), who began working on the typeface for Monotype in 1932, three years before he came to settle in Britain. After a brief period of internment (in Australia) as a foreign national, Wolpe joined the UK publishing house Faber and Faber in 1941, where he remained until his retirement in 1975.

During his time at Faber, Wolpe demonstrated the versatility and authority of the Albertus typeface whatever the subject matter – poetry, food, history, theory, and art, ancient and modern. And, despite Albertus's strong association with Faber, the typeface has played many roles – on TV (*Zoo Quest*, *Secret Army*, *Restless*, and, in modified form, for the cult 1960s series *The Prisoner*); in the logo for UK imprint Picador; and on music packaging for Joy Division and New Order (designed by Peter Saville) and even Coldplay. Albertus was also used in some of the 'blue plaques' installed by the London County Council; on street nameplates in Lambeth, where Wolpe lived; and in wayfinding signs made for the City of London.

A page from *David Bowie Is* (2013), designed by Jon Abbott at Barnbrook. The book was published to accompany the record-breaking exhibition devoted to the musician's life, work and costumes at the Victoria and Albert Museum, London.

abcdefghi123
LMNO,.£%"

DAVID BOWIE IS TURNING US ALL INTO VOYEURS

PEIGNOT
Cassandre's footnote

1937
A M Cassandre for
Deberny & Peignot

A M Cassandre's Peignot is an odd footnote in the history of type design; it reverses the Bauhaus-era rejection of authoritarian capitals with a typeface whose lower case is mainly made of upper-case letterforms, with a few ascenders and descenders thrown in to aid reading. The original specimen claimed that lower-case letters 'will soon come to seem as archaic as the shapes of Gothic [i.e. black-letter] characters'.

Charles Peignot (of the French foundry Deberny & Peignot) himself promoted the new typeface to British printers and designers at an event in London, during which he showed a film about it and gave a speech about the qualities of Cassandre's creation – 'the fruit of ten years' work'. Cassandre (1901–68) is best known as the pre-eminent French poster artist of his day, the designer-illustrator behind archetypal campaigns for Dubonnet, Nord Express and many more.

According to the manifesto-like original specimen, the Peignot letters were conceived as 'engraved' rather than 'written'. 'The essential forms', it thundered, 'are not either of scribble or that embellished form of it known as calligraphy.' In this respect, Peignot (the typeface) was a slight return to ninth-century manuscript capitals – a time before scribes came along and spoiled everything with their 'scribbles'.

Peignot was never a huge commercial success, but its off-kilter, pre-postmodern mood has proved to be popular and/or effective with users as different as Gary Larson (*The Far Side*) and in-car air freshener manufacturers Magic Tree.

The first non-promotional use of Peignot appears to have been for an edition (1938) of Oscar Wilde's *Salomé* for the Limited Editions Club designed by René ben Sussan, who set the stage directions and dialogue in the typeface.

AbcdefghijkI2
LMNO,.£%*"

Salomé (se levant). Vous me donnerez tout ce que je demanderai, tétrarque ?

Hérodias. Ne dansez pas, ma fille.

Hérode. Tout, fût-ce la moitié de mon royaume.

Salomé. Vous le jurez, tétrarque ?

Hérode. Je le jure, Salomé.

Hérodias. Ma fille, ne dansez pas.

Salomé. Sur quoi jurez-vous, tétrarque ?

Hérode. Sur ma vie, sur ma couronne, sur mes dieux. Tout ce que vous voudrez je vous le donnerai, fût-ce la moitié de mon royaume, si vous dansez pour moi. Oh ! Salomé, Salomé, dansez pour moi.

Salomé. Vous avez juré, tétrarque.

Hérode. J'ai juré, Salomé.

Salomé. Tout ce que je vous demanderai, fût-ce la moitié de votre royaume.

Hérodias. Ne dansez pas, ma fille.

Hérode. Fût-ce la moitié de mon royaume. Comme reine, tu serais très belle, Salomé, s'il te plaisait de demander la moitié de mon royaume. N'est-ce pas qu'elle serait très belle comme reine ?... Ah ! il fait froid ici ! il y a un vent très froid, et j'entends... pourquoi est-ce que j'entends dans l'air

PLAYBILL
Posters: stick 'em up!

1938
Robert Harling for
Stephenson Blake

This is a thick, condensed typeface with thick slab serifs, based on the kind of jobbing font that can be seen on Victorian theatre and circus posters. Robert Harling (1910–2008), its designer, is one of those extraordinary people who had several careers – in advertising and design, newspapers and magazines, and as a sailor, a spy and a novelist – but he was also a considerable self-mythologizer. He edited the magazines *Typography*, published by James Shand's Shenval Press, and *Alphabet and Image*.

Harling's enthusiasm as a collector of ephemera spilled into his type designs: Playbill uses the forms of theatrical poster wood types – the so-called Antiques – that were popularly used to promote Victorian music-hall events. However, they were also strongly associated with the Wild West – the types used for 'Wanted' posters – and Playbill still has an active life in the movie industry, where their exaggerated slab serifs produce what poster collector and academic Paul Rennie calls 'a distinctive optical dazzle and visual punch'.

Poster for Sergio Leone's Spaghetti Western *Once Upon a Time in the West* (1968). The original Italian title *C'era una volta il West* is set in the Playbill typeface, a 20th-century re-imagining of the 19th century like the Western movie genre itself.

abcdefghijk123
LMNO,.£%*"

EURO INTERNATIONAL FILMS presenta

IL PIU' SPETTACOLARE WESTERN DI TUTTI I TEMPI

C'ERA UNA VOLTA IL WEST

REGIA DI SERGIO LEONE _ HENRY FONDA CLAUDIA CARDINALE JASON ROBARDS
GABRIELE FERZETTI CHARLES BRONSON NEL RUOLO DI ARMONICA PAOLO STOPPA
E IN ORDINE ALFABETICO
TECHNICOLOR TECHNISCOPE JACK ELAM LIONEL STANDER WOODY STRODE FRANK WOLFF KEENAN WYNN UNA PRODUZIONE RAFRAN - S.MARCO

MISTRAL
The script that stuck around

1953
Roger Excoffon for
Fonderie Olive

To many type designers, Roger Excoffon's Mistral is a thing of wonder – a handwriting typeface with an elegance that can make a line of printed type appear to have flown directly from the hand of a cultured Frenchman. Each casually sloping character links securely with the one before it and the one that follows. Yet Mistral was produced during the last years of metal typeface design. Making letters that could run together in a convincing rhythmic fashion presented huge technical problems in addition to the aesthetic challenges. Script typefaces had been around, if little used, since the seventeenth century, but Mistral, based on informal, everyday handwriting, was a breakthrough.

As a type designer, Excoffon (1910–83) was a late starter, who turned his hand to type design when his brother-in-law, Marcel Olive, asked him to become the artistic director of the family firm soon after World War II. Though Excoffon was relatively inexperienced, he quickly produced a series of popular display faces – Banco, Mistral, Choc, Calypso, Antique – that helped put Fonderie Olive on the map.

Mistral was an aesthetic and a technical triumph, too, and adapted easily to later manufacturing and distribution methods: photosetting, rubdowns (such as Letraset) and digital.

In recent years the technical possibilities of digital design, which permit huge freedom in the way letters swoop and swirl and overlap with each other, have liberated script type design, an area in which the Argentinian Alejandro Paul is one of the most prolific designers. Scripts now form one of the fastest-growing areas of the type market.

Examples of Mistral photographed by Matt Soar in Montréal, Canada, between 2003 and 2007 include businesses devoted to videos (Le Super Club), pet food (Club K-9 Plus) and fashion (Quelles Sensations and Chelsea).

abcdefghijk123
lmno,.£%*"

HELVETICA
The blue jeans typeface

1957
Max Miedinger for Haas

Helvetica was a crisp new spin on a jobbing grotesque (its original name was Neue Haas Grotesk) that hit the market at exactly the right time. That it has become one of the most famous and recognizable typefaces is regarded by many as a historical accident – the result of supply and demand and astute marketing by the Haas foundry at a time when Swiss Modernism was transforming the postwar industrial world.

Many designers love it. And many more regard it as boring but useful, or so bland and predictable that they can't face using it. Helvetica appeared to conquer the contemporary world at some time in the 1960s, and remains the default corporate typeface for any number of businesses. Some designers hate it with a passion. Its bland ubiquity inspired Erik Spiekermann to devise Meta (see page 94) as an alternative. For Pentagram's Paula Scher it represents the industrial-military complex that her generation rebelled against at the time of the Vietnam War. Yet, for Scher's Pentagram colleague Michael Bierut, Helvetica is a typeface that instantly makes anything using it look clean, efficient and modern.

Both these observations were made in Gary Hustwit's indie documentary *Helvetica* (2007), which intercuts designers' observations with *verité* footage of the typeface in everyday streetscapes – it is difficult to travel anywhere in the world without seeing Helvetica used for something. This is one reason why the Amsterdam design company Experimental Jetset describes Helvetica as 'the Beatles of typefaces', while Univers designer Adrian Frutiger talks of it as the 'blue jeans' typeface.

Posters for Milan's Piccolo Teatro designed by Massimo Vignelli, 1964–6. A master of Helvetica, Vignelli also famously used it for his signs for the New York Subway system and his logo for American Airlines, demonstrating the typeface at its brutal best.

abcdefg123 LMNO,.£%"

Piccolo Teatro di Milano

Ente Autonomo

Direzione Paolo Grassi - Giorgio Strehler

Milano - Palazzo del Broletto - Via Rovello, 2
Telefoni: 803464 - 8690631/2/3/4
Biglietteria 872352 - 877663

20° anno dell'Ente
stagione 1966/67
al Teatro Lirico

Via Larga, 14
telefoni: 866418 - 876889

da giovedì
24 novembre

tutte le sere alle ore 21,10 precise
domeniche e festivi alle 15,30 e 21,10
lunedì (esclusi festivi e prefestivi) riposo

spettacolo in abbonamento tagliando n. 1

I Giganti
della montagna

Mito in due tempi di Luigi Pirandello

diretto da Giorgio Strehler

distribuzione:

La compagnia della Contessa:

Ilse, detta ancora La Contessa
Il Conte, suo marito
Diamante, la seconda donna
Cromo, il Caratterista
Spizzi, l'Attor Giovine
Battaglia, generico-donna
Sacerdote
Lumachi, col carretto
Cotrone, detto Il Mago

Valentina Cortese
Luciano Alberici
Marisa Fabbri
Mario Carotenuto
Alessandro Ninchi
Virgilio Gottardi
Leopoldo Valentini
Pietro Buttarelli
Turi Ferro

Gli scalognati:

Il Nano Quaquèo
Duccio Doccia
La Sgricia
Milordino
Mara Mara
Maddalena

Lino Robi
Olimpo Griggio
Nuccia Fumo
Carlo Formigoni
Dory Dorika
Ivana Monti

Fantocci:

Giovanni Brusadori
Giorgio Caldarelli
Claudio Caramaschi
Costantino Carrozza
Rosalia De Francisci
Guglielmo Ferraiola
Maria Teresa Letizia
Mirka Martini
Emy Rossi Scotti

Tempo e luogo, indeterminati:
al limite, fra la favola e la realtà.

Scene di Ezio Frigerio
Costumi di Ezio Frigerio - Enrico Job
Musiche di Fiorenzo Carpi
realizzate dal complesso di Raoul Ceroni

Maschere di Luisa Spinatelli
realizzate da Carlo Schiavon
Movimenti mimici a cura di Marise Flach
Regista assistente: Raffaele Maiello
Assistenti alla regia: Francesco Carnelutti -
Klaus Michael Grüber - Alberto Negrin

Le scene sono realizzate dal Laboratorio
di Scenografia del Piccolo Teatro
Pittore scenografo Leonardo Ricchelli
Costruttore Bruno Colombo
Il velluto del palco è del Cotonificio Legler
Attrezzeria: Rancati - Milano

I costumi sono realizzati dalla Sartoria
del Piccolo Teatro
Capitecnici: Angelo Bocenti - Alice Brugnaro -
Ines Rezzonico
Collaboratrice: Monica Hasse
Il costume della signora Valentina Cortese
è realizzato dalla Sartoria Valentino
Parrucche:Severgnini Milano - Maggi Roma
Calzature: Pedrazzoli - Milano

Direttori di palcoscenico: Giancarlo Fortunato -
Mario Baldini
Realizzatore delle luci: Mino Campolmi

Rammentatore: Cesare Frigerio
Primo macchinista: Fortunato Michieli
Sarta di palcoscenico: Mina Maestrini

Prezzi:

2800 Poltrona di platea	1800 Poltroncina di platea	1200 Balconata

La prenotazioni si ricevono alla biglietteria
del Teatro Lirico (tel. 876889 - 866418)
ogni giorno dalle ore 10 alle ore 20.
La vendita e la prenotazione dei posti
vengono aperte con quattro giorni di anticipo.

I posti prenotati telefonicamente si ritengono
rinunciati se non vengono ritirati entro le ore 18
del giorno successivo alla prenotazione.
Servizio di recapito a domicilio dei biglietti
prenotati telefonicamente.
I prezzi sui esposti includono ingresso e tasse.

Il Teatro non può morire

Forma della vita stessa, tutti ne siamo attori;
e abolito o abbandonati i teatri, il teatro seguiterebbe
nella vita, insopprimibile; e sarebbe sempre spettacolo
la natura stessa delle cose. Parlare di morte del
teatro in un tempo come il nostro così pieno
di contrasti e dunque così ricco di materia
drammatica, in una così grande varietà di dubbi,
tanto fermento di passioni e succedersi

di casi che commuovono la intera vita dei popoli,
urto di eventi e instabilità di situazioni e il bisogno
sempre più di tutti avvertito d'affermare alla fine
qualche certezza nuova in mezzo a un così
angoscioso andegiare di dubbi,
è veramente un non senso.

Luigi Pirandello (dal Discorso al convegno Volta
sul teatro drammatico, ottobre 1934)

Piccolo Teatro di Milano

Ente Autonomo

Direzione: Paolo Grassi - Giorgio Strehler

Milano - Palazzo del Broletto - Via Rovello, 2
Telefoni:
Direzione 896915 - 865464
Biglietteria 872352 - 877663

Ufficio Abbonamenti e Propaganda
Via Rovello, 6
Telefoni 873505 - 867206

diciottesimo anno dell'Ente

diciannovesima dalla fondazione

stagione 1964/65
al Teatro Lirico
al Piccolo Teatro

Le baruffe chiozzotte

regia di Giorgio Strehler

di Carlo Goldoni

Sul caso di J. Robert Oppenheimer

allestimento di Giorgio Strehler
e Claré Carpi, Enrico Job, Gigi Lunari Virginia Puecher,
Fulvio Tolusso

di Heinar Kipphardt
prima rappresentazione in Italia

Il Signor di Pourceaugnac

regia di Eduardo De Filippo

di Molière
nuova traduzione di Ruggero Jacobbi

Il gioco dei potenti
da Enrico VI

regia di Giorgio Strehler

Parti I - V - III
di William Shakespeare

La lanzichenecca

regia di Virginia Puecher

di Vincenzo Di Mattia
novità assoluta

Il Mistero

regia di Orazio Costa

della Natività, Passione e Resurrezione di Nostro Signore

laudi medioevali dei Secoli XIII e XIV
riunite ed elaborate da Silvio D'Amico

L'anima buona di Sezuan

regia di Giorgio Strehler

di Bertolt Brecht

Parteciperanno agli spettacoli, tra gli altri, i seguenti attori
(per ordine alfabetico)

Luciano Alberici, Armando Alzelmo, Manuela Andrei,
Gastone Bartolucci, Ugo Bologna, Narciso Bonati, Paolo Borboni,
Giulio Brogi, Tino Buazzelli, Pietro Buttarelli,
Giancarlo Cajo, Paride Calonghi, Lino Capolicchio,
Donatella Ceccarello, Ivan Cecchini, Umberto Ceriani,
Valentina Cortese, Elio Crovetto,
Renato De Carmine, Sandro Dori, Attilio Duse,
Ottavio Fanfani,

Gianni Garco, Guido Gheduzzi, Gabriella Giacobbe,
Raffaele Giangrande, Giulio Girola, Virgilio Gottardi, Carlo Gravina,
Franco Graziosi,
Anna Nivoltri, Mario Mariani, Gianfranco Mauri,
Corrado Nardi, Domenico Negri,
Ilario Occhini, Glauco Onorato,
Corrado Pani, Nico Pepe,
Tino Scotti, Franco Sportelli,
Ferdinando Tamberlani, Marco Tulli,
Mario Valdemarin, Lino Volonghi.

Scene e costumi di Tullio Costa, Luciano Damiani, Enrico Job,
Mino Maccari, Carlo Tommasi,
Musiche di Fiorenzo Carpi, Raoul Ceroni, Paul Dessau, Gino Negri
Regista assistente: Fulvio Tolusso,
Maestro di danze: Fulvio Tolusso,
Maestra di mimo: Marise Flach,
Assistenti alla regia: Klaus Michael Grüber, Alberto Negrin, Paolo Radaelli,

Capo del servizi tecnici: Bruno Colombo
Direttori di palcoscenico: Bruno Martini, Giancarlo Fortunato,
Vice direttori di palcoscenico: Luciano Ferroni, Nino Monta,
Capo elettricista: Gaetano Camperini,
Realizzatore delle luci: Mino Campolmi,
Rammentatori: Cesare Frigerio, Giuseppe Lalio,
Attrezzerie: Aldo Dal Sasso,
Sarte di palcoscenico: Mina Maestrini, Lea Gardnelli,
Secondo parrucchiere: Ildebrando Biribò,
Realizzazioni scenografiche: Laboratorio di scenografia
del Piccolo Teatro di Milano,
Pittore scenografo: Leonardo Ricchelli,
Costruttore: Bruno Colombo,
Confezione dei costumi: Sartoria del Piccolo Teatro di Milano,
Capitecnici: Angelo Bocenti, Tino Micoletti, Ines Rezzonico,

ABBONAMENTO A 6 SPETTACOLI
il cui due di spettacoli nella alternative proposte

6500 Poltrona di platea	4200 Poltroncina di platea	3300 Balconata

Nell'abbonamento ad ogni ordine di posti è compreso:
Tagliando n. 1 per « Le Baruffe Chiozzotte »
Tagliando n. 2 per « Sul caso di J. Robert Oppenheimer »
Tagliando n. 3 ove il giovco dei potenti è obbligato scegliere tra:
« Sul caso di J. Robert Oppenheimer » o « Il Signor di Pourceaugnac »
Tagliando n. 4 per il giovco dei potenti » (da « Enrico VI »)
Tagliando n. 5 ove è obbligato scegliere tra:
« La Lanzichenecca » o « L'anima buona di Sezuan »
Tagliando n. 6 per « Il Mistero »

Diritto di prenotazione preventiva gratuita da comunicare al botteghino
del Teatro col la spettacolo si riferisce
direttamente il giorno del Piccolo Teatro.

L'abbonamento dà diritto ad assistere ad una sola qualsiasi
alle sei prime, compatibilmente con le disponibilità della sala,
nel solo rispetto feriali, prefestive, festive, diurne e serali.

La scelta dello spettacolo non alternativo
è per abbonamento può essere proposta e sostituita,
per eventuali cause di forza maggiore,
gli spettacoli in abbonamento si realizzano uno o più in altre sedi.

Per qualsiasi altra informazione è per ogni chiarimento,
gli interessati sono designati all'Ufficio Abbonamenti del Piccolo Teatro,
Via Rovello 6 - telefoni 873.505 - 867.206.

La Direzione del Piccolo Teatro si riserva di spostare e sostituire,
per eventuali cause di forza maggiore,
gli spettacoli in abbonamento realizzandone uno o più in altre sedi.

I prezzi di abbonamento sono comprensivi di ingressi e tasse.

UNIVERS
Cornerstone of Swiss typography

1952–60
Adrian Frutiger for
Deberny & Peignot

Univers, from the French foundry Deberny & Peignot, was one of the first examples of a systematic type family, organized by weight and size, and it remains a favourite of Modernist designers worldwide. Adrian Frutiger (1928–) was born in Switzerland, and his ambitious project, with its 21 numbered versions laid out in a grid reminiscent of the periodic table, remains a high point of Modernist type design. The numbers refer to each font's weight and width.

Its early champion (in the pages of *Typografische Monatsblätter* and his 1967 textbook *Typographie*) was Emil Ruder, who used the typeface with great skill and delicacy. Despite the machine-age rigour of its conception, designed for the then cutting-edge technology of photosetting, Univers has an elegance that makes it popular with designers who baulk at the more rough-hewn functionalism of Helvetica. Emil Ruder, who for many years taught at the Basel School of Design, was an early advocate: he and his students helped make this typeface family a cornerstone of Swiss typographic excellence.

Frutiger conceived the idea of a whole system of sans-serif fonts in his early twenties. He recalls that when he showed Charles Peignot his rough star-shaped assembly of 16 variations 'he almost jumped in the air: "Good heavens, Adrian, that's the future!"'

This 1954 specimen (recreated by Untitled and Jonathan Christie) for 21 members of the Univers family demonstrates its system of weights and widths with a grid partly influenced by the periodic table of the elements.

abcdefg123
LMNO,.£%"

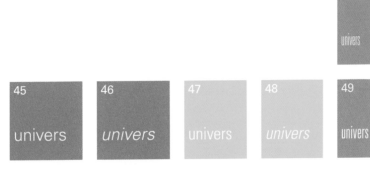

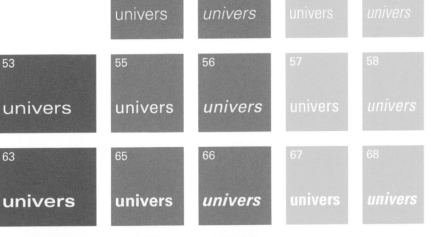

TRANSPORT
House style for Britain

1957–63
Jock Kinneir &
Margaret Calvert

Transport was designed for a specific purpose, for Britain's new motorway signs in the late 1950s. The new company of ex-DRU (Design Research Unit) designer Jock Kinneir (1917–94) and his young assistant Margaret Calvert (1936–) worked on a comprehensive programme of type and pictogram design, which they then applied to the entire British road system. Several foundries produced versions of the Transport typeface. Originally designed in two weights: medium and heavy – the latter reads better when the letters are white out of a colour or black. The Kinneir–Calvert system of type and pictograms has been influential on an international scale.

Signs in Transport dominate the British urban landscape. With a very British take on International Modernism, the typeface is always telling Brits where to go. This was not lost on GOV.UK's Ben Terrett, when his GDS (Government Digital Service) design team embarked on a major overhaul of the nation's official website. Government websites are required to be as accessible as possible, and the major component is written information, from birth certificates to death via taxes and visas. The GDS design of GOV.UK was the overall winner of the Design Museum's Designs of the Year Awards in 2013.

The webfont used by GOV.UK is a version of Transport that Danish designer Henrik Kubel of of A2/SW/HK made with the typeface's original co-designer Margaret Calvert. Entitled New Transport, it is in two weights, light and bold, for the government site, but will eventually be released as a big family.

After the motorway signage had been rolled out across the nation, Jock Kinneir and Margaret Calvert were commissioned to design new signage for all of Britain's major roads.

abcdefg123
LMNO,.£%"

ANTIQUE OLIVE
France's alternative national typeface

Roger Excoffon for
Fonderie Olive

This typeface takes its name from Fonderie Olive, the independent French foundry inherited by Marcel Olive, who commissioned a series of designs from the audacious type designer Roger Excoffon (1910–83). This 1954 specimen (recreated by Untitled and Johnathan Christie) for 21 members of the Univers family demonstrates its system of weights and widths with a grid partly influenced by the periodic table of the elements. The origins of Antique Olive lie in some experimental drawings that Excoffon made with a view to improving the legibility of sans serifs.

When the new wave of sans-serif type designs (see Helvetica and Univers, pages 70–73) burst upon the scene in the late 1950s, Fonderie Olive published Antique Olive in response. Though it never achieved the international success of Helvetica or Univers, Antique Olive soon became what the designer Gerard Unger described as an 'alternative national typeface' for France – you can see it all over the nation on shopfronts and in advertising materials. In its bold form the typeface it is known as Compact while the extra bold weight is called Nord (actually released separately before Antique Olive), which was for many years the typeface used by Air France.

Cover of the first specimen for Antique Olive published by Fonderie Olive, 1960. Antique Olive was the last typeface in France designed to be cast as metal foundry type for hand setting. Although its designer, Roger Excoffon, sought to establish a new mode of type for reading, Antique Olive's lasting success was as display type for posters, cafés and shopfronts...

abcdefg12
LMNO,.£%*

une antique nouvelle de la fonderie Olive

SABON
Tschichold's parting gift

Leipzig-born Jan Tschichold (1902–74) was one of the most significant figures in twentieth-century typography. In the 1920s his groundbreaking 'Elementare Typographie' issue (1925) of *Typographische Mitteilungen* and his book *Die neue Typographie* (1928) demonstrated the relevance of European Modernism (of the Bauhaus and beyond) to practical typography. Tschichold's theoretical writings were balanced by practice – exemplary poster and book design. In the 1933 he left Nazi Germany for Switzerland, where he completed another influential book, *Typographische Gestaltung* (1935), and designed books for Birkhäuser.

From 1947 to 1949 Tschichold was employed by the founder of Penguin Books, Allen Lane. Working through every title published to date, he carried out a thorough overhaul of Penguin's typography, writing the famous 'Penguin Composition Rules'. According to his biographer Ruari McLean, Tschichold did 'more, in three years, than any other single book designer had done'.

The typeface Sabon is a monument to Tschichold's belief in the ability of typography to improve the everyday. It was designed, in a commission from several German master printers, to work across several formats: hot-metal casting (Linotype or Monotype) and hand composition, though its release came as the old technology was dying. Sabon was based on a design by Claude Garamont, and its italic based on a font by Robert Granjon. The name comes from French type founder Jacques Sabon, whose widow married Frankfurt type founder Konrad Berner – Tschichold found a starting point for the design in one of Berner's specimen sheets.

Details from a specimen brochure entitled *Sabon-Antiqua* published by D. Stempel, c.1970s.

abcdefghij123
LMNO,.£%"

Das Ziel der Harmonisierung war es, eine Drucktype zu schaffen, die es ermöglicht, den Maschinensatz beider Systeme und den Handsatz beliebig auszutauschen oder zu kombinieren. Das verlangt eine formengleiche, in Bildgröße und Schriftweite identische Schrift, die mit der Sabon-Antiqua erstmals in der Schriftgeschichte erreicht wurde. Einem Satzbild aus der Sabon ist es nicht anzusehen, in welchem der drei Setzverfahren es hergestellt ist. Das Bemerkenswerte dabei ist, daß die Forderung und Erfüllung der Identität für diese neue Schrift in allen drei Setzverfahren zu der optimal möglichen Lösung geführt haben. Die Sabon-Antiqua steht in vollendeten Proportionen ebenbürtig neben den besten Schriftschöpfungen früherer Jahrhunderte.

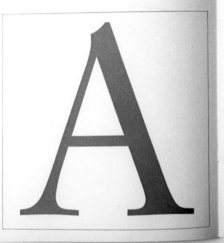

Linotype-Satz
Deutlich beweist der Vergleich dieser Satzbeispiele die Formengleichheit der Buchstaben, den gleichen Breitenverlauf der drei Garnituren und die Übereinstimmung des Schriftbildes in allen drei Setzverfahren.
Monotype-Satz
Deutlich beweist der Vergleich dieser Satzbeispiele die Formengleichheit der Buchstaben, den gleichen Breitenverlauf der drei Garnituren und die Übereinstimmung des Schriftbildes in allen drei Setzverfahren.
Handsatz
Deutlich beweist der Vergleich dieser Satzbeispiele die Formengleichheit der Buchstaben, den gleichen Breitenverlauf der drei Garnituren und die Übereinstimmung des Schriftbildes in allen drei Setzverfahren.
›Linotype-Satz
Deutlich beweist der Vergleich dieser Satzbeispiele die Formengleichheit der Buchstaben, den gleichen Breitenverlauf der drei Garnituren und die Übereinstimmung des Schriftbildes in allen drei Setzverfahren.
Monotype-Satz
Deutlich beweist der Vergleich dieser Satzbeispiele die Formengleichheit der Buchstaben, den gleichen Breitenverlauf der drei Garnituren und die Übereinstimmung des Schriftbildes in allen drei Setzverfahren.
Handsatz
Deutlich beweist der Vergleich dieser Satzbeispiele die Formengleichheit der Buchstaben, den gleichen Breitenverlauf der drei Garnituren und die Übereinstimmung des Schriftbildes in allen drei Setzverfahren.
›Linotype-Satz
Deutlich beweist der Vergleich dieser Satzbeispiele die Formengleichheit der Buchstaben, den gleichen Breitenverlauf der drei Garnituren und die Übereinstimmung des Schriftbildes in allen drei Setzverfahren.
›Monotype-Satz
Deutlich beweist der Vergleich dieser Satzbeispiele die Formengleichheit der Buchstaben, den gleichen Breitenverlauf der drei Garnituren und die Übereinstimmung des Schriftbildes in allen drei Setzverfahren.
Handsatz
Deutlich beweist der Vergleich dieser Satzbeispiele die Formengleichheit der Buchstaben, den gleichen Breitenverlauf der drei Garnituren und die Übereinstimmung des Schriftbildes in allen drei Setzverfahren.

Nur ein erfahrener Typograph und Schriftkenner von Rang konnte mit einer so bedeutenden und schwierigen Aufgabe betraut werden. Die Wahl fiel auf Jan Tschichold, der sich bei der Entwurfsarbeit auf reiche Kenntnisse und ein gründliches Quellenstudium historischer Schriften – im besonderen Maße der Garamondtypen – stützen konnte. Das gesamte Schaffen Tschicholds weist ihn darüber hinaus als feinsinnigen Buchgestalter und Typographen aus. In Anerkennung seines Werkes erhielt er im Jahre 1954 die Goldmedaille des American Institute of Graphic Arts, und die Royal Society of Arts in London verlieh ihm 1965 die Würde eines Honorary Royal Designer for Industry. Beim Entwurf der Sabon kam Tschichold auch zustatten, daß er mit den Besonderheiten aller drei Setzverfahren gut vertraut ist. Die meisterhaften Zeichnungen und der Ausfall der gesamten Schrift zeigen Tschicholds schriftkundiges Wissen und seine Form- und Stilsicherheit bis in die feinsten Details. In der Sabon-Antiqua hat seine jahrzehntelange Beschäftigung mit der Schrift ihre Krönung gefunden. Schon heute liegen Urteile von hervorragenden Schriftkennern des In- und Auslandes vor, die dieser Schrift eine große Zukunft voraussagen.

6
Der Werdegang Jakob Sabons als Schriftschneider ist unbekannt. Seine Herkunft aus Lyon verbindet sich unwillkürlich mit dem Gedanken an die beste Schriftschneider-Tradition Frankreichs. Robert Granjon wirkte in Lyon; es wäre denkbar, daß Sabon noch in seiner Heimat mit ihm zusammengetroffen ist, aber wir

8
Der Werdegang Jakob Sabons als Schriftschneider ist unbekannt. Seine Herkunft aus Lyon verbindet sich unwillkürlich mit dem Gedanken an die beste Schriftschneider-Tradition Frankreichs. Robert Granjon wirkte in Lyon; es wäre denkbar, daß Sabon noch in seiner Heimat mit ihm zusammengetroffen ist, aber wir

9
Der Werdegang Jakob Sabons als Schriftschneider ist unbekannt. Seine Herkunft aus Lyon verbindet sich unwillkürlich mit dem Gedanken an die beste Schriftschneider-Tradition Frankreichs. Robert Granjon wirkte in Lyon; es wäre denkbar, daß Sabon noch in seiner Heimat mit ihm zusammengetroffen ist, aber wir

10
Der Werdegang Jakob Sabons als Schriftschneider ist unbekannt. Seine Herkunft aus Lyon verbindet sich unwillkürlich mit dem Gedanken an die beste Schriftschneider-Tradition Frankreichs. Robert Granjon wirkte in Lyon; es wäre denkbar, daß Sabon noch in seiner Heimat mit ihm zusammengetroffen ist, aber wir

12
Der Werdegang Jakob Sabons als Schriftschneider ist unbekannt. Seine Herkunft aus Lyon verbindet sich unwillkürlich mit dem Gedanken an die beste Schriftschneider-Tradition Frankreichs. Robert Granjon wirkte in Lyon; es wäre denkbar, daß Sabon noch in seiner Heimat mit ihm zusammengetroffen ist, aber wir

NEW ALPHABET
The shock of the New Alphabet

1967
Wim Crouwel

The original New Alphabet, designed by Total Design's Wim Crouwel (1928–) for the twenty-third edition of the Kwadraat-Bladen series of 'square magazines' made by the Dutch printer Steendrukkerij de Jong & Co, was a provocation rather than a workable typeface. Crouwel considered the impact of technology, in particular television's cathode ray tube (CRT) on type forms, and devised an alphabet made purely from vertical and horizontal lines.

Though barely legible in conventional terms, in Crouwel's elegantly designed booklet (which also included NASA images) the New Alphabet came to stand for uncompromising, space-age modernity. The typeface was used, with some modifications, when Peter Saville designed the sleeve for Joy Division's *Unknown Pleasures* (1979), while in the late 1990s, with Crouwel's approval, British designers Freda Sack and David Quay produced an extended digital version.

Like Crouwel himself, the original New Alphabet was controversial in the Netherlands and, in subsequent Kwadraat editions, prompted responses from Gerard Unger (issue no. 24) and Anthon Beeke (issue no. 28), who devised a Baskerville-like alphabet made entirely from the bodies of naked women.

Crouwel is now regarded (in the UK at least) as a late twentieth-century design hero. His 'canonization' was further advanced when superfan Tony Brook (of Spin) curated a vast, white-walled exhibition (2011) of his work for London's Design Museum.

Wim Crouwel with a New Alphabet rug, designed by Tony Brook as a particularly extravagant souvenir (price £1608) of an exhibition devoted to Crouwel's work, which was held at London's Design Museum in 2011.

ZAPF DINGBATS
The alphabet that wasn't

1978
Hermann Zapf for ITC

Printers' typecases have always included non-alphabetical elements – asterisks, daggers, fists, pilcrows and other symbols or pictograms, used to aid the meaning and clarity of running text or just to make it look pretty. The earliest characters may have been the *hedera* (ivy leaf), the *manicule* (pointing hand) and the printer's flower (or *fleuron*). Over the centuries printers have routinely supplied type elements that could be combined to make decorative borders or illustrative patterns, according to the fashions and needs of the day, not to mention the thick rectangles, triangles, circles and rules that added punch to Futurist and Dada publications in the early twentieth century.

Zapf Dingbats was named for its German designer, Hermann Zapf (1918–) and marked the moment when the computer keyboard became a means of selecting a slew of symbols, squiggles and other marks. The typeface, which many might argue is not a typeface at all, achieved widespread use in the mid-1980s when it was bundled with the very limited selection of typefaces on Apple's series of LaserWriter printers. It has drilled its way into public consciousness ever since.

In recent years technology has made possible a fantastical array of new 'typefaces' that combine pattern-making and illustration with the tools and delivery methods of digital type design. Kapitza's Blossomy (2005), Emigre's ZeitGuys (by Bob Auldfish and Eric Donelan, 1994) and Martin Friedl's Poppi (2003) are just a few of such creations, but Zapf Dingbats endure.

In early desktop publishing, Dingbats made life easier for editors and designers who needed to insert 'bullet points' in lists or tick boxes in forms. There were symbols for stub pencils, pen nibs, ticks, crosses – even an Apple logo. Hermann Zapf originally designed more than a thousand symbols, which ITC edited down to 360.

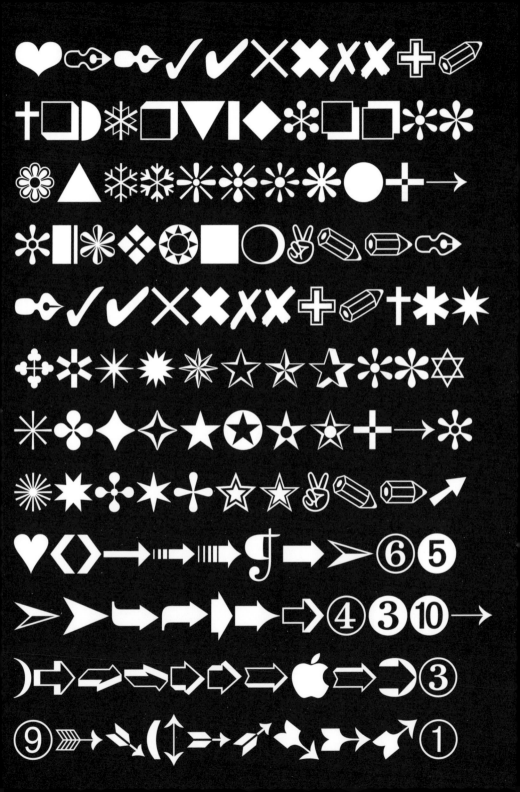

BELL CENTENNIAL
Type as information

1978
Matthew Carter

This immensely practical typeface, originally commissioned for the centenary of the AT&T phonebook in the United States, has had a versatile second life as an 'expressive' or 'new wave' typeface. The phone company's original brief was for a face that could be read when printed on the directory's rough paper at the tiny size of six points. The British-born designer Matthew Carter (1937–) based his type family on Bell Gothic (originally designed in-house at Linotype in 1938), creating four weights – 'Address', 'Name & Number', 'Bold Listing' and 'Sub-Caption' – that define the hierarchy of the information they list.

The idiosyncratic notches in the letterforms, which become quite startling when shown at large sizes, come from Carter's problem-solving approach to reproduction and printing technology. When CRT (Cathode Ray Typesetting) technology was applied to the earlier typeface, Bell Gothic (which worked fine in the old hot-metal methods) became overly light, and degraded.

Carter realized this could be fixed by putting more ink on the printing plate, but this produced legibility issues in a more conventional face – the small letterforms clogged up with ink. Carter compensated for this by designing Bell Centennial with notched openings at the typeface's junctions. To achieve this, he had to design each letter pixel by pixel, an enormously time-consuming task.

This giant letter 'N' (right) demonstrates the 'ink traps' (marked by the pink circles) that stop the letters of Bell Centennial filling up with ink when they are printed at small sizes on the low-quality paper of a telephone directory (below). Many designers have made use of the dream-like qualities of using such a Lilliputian typeface at Brobdingnagian size.

abcdefg123
LMNO,.£"

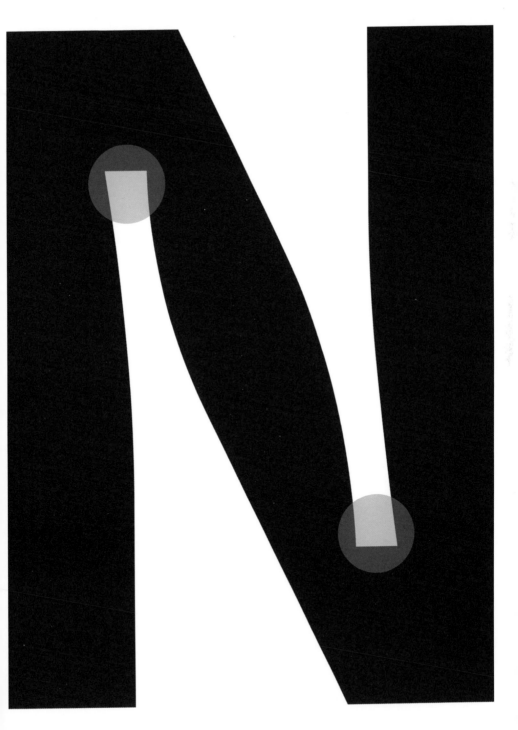

BEOWOLF
Teaching computers to fail

1989
LettError

Few recent typefaces can claim to be as radical – anarchistic, even – as Beowolf, a digital typeface by Just van Rossum (1966–) and Erik van Blokland (1967–) that subverted the still-new software of PostScript to be deliberately inconsistent. The typographer who sets a word or sentence in Beowolf can have no idea what will emerge from the studio's laser printer. What comes back from another printer, or the repro house, will be something different again – it's a sorcerer's apprentice of a typeface, running amok in the operating system of the user's computer.

The 'distressed' typeface has been part of graphic design for generations, whether from copying the imperfections of age or unpredictable printing conditions. Designers have always found many and varied ways to change and distort type – whether by stretching it on rubber (Massin), or projecting it on to a human body (Brownjohn) – and LettError's Beowolf chimes well with the deconstructive and postmodern type and typography of its era. Yet the distortions of Vaughan Oliver's lettering on 4AD sleeves, the cacophony of David Carson's *Ray Gun* spreads (1992–9), and the spiky aggression of, say, Frank Heine's Amplifier (1994) or Mark Andresen's Not Caslon (1991) can still be marshalled precisely by typographers. Beowolf, true to its almost-namesake Beowulf, remains an uncaged beast, and in its ingenious subversion of digital code the typeface anticipates the process-driven and interactive design of the twenty-first century.

Beowolf on the cover of *Eye* magazine no. 7 vol. 2 1992, a typography special issue, which includes Robin Kinross's prophetic overview 'The digital wave'. Cover design by Stephen Coates. 'The modern font format just does not allow for such silliness,' writes Van Blokland on the LettError website, but you can buy a post-postmodern version in OpenType format, and you can see the original in the collection at MoMA (the Museum of Modern Art) in New York.

abcdefghi12
LMNO,.£%*"

THE INTERNATIONAL REVIEW OF GRAPHIC DESIGN No 7 VOL. 2 1992

TYPOGRAPHY SPECIAL ISSUE

eye

TRAJAN
Set in stone

1989
Carol Twombly
for Adobe

Trajan evokes a time long before type. This digital typeface, created by Carol Twombly (1959–) when she was one of two in-house designers at the fast-growing tech company Adobe, is a historical revival that goes back to the second century CE. The original Trajan Column was erected in Rome (113 CE) to celebrate the military achievements of the Roman emperor whose name it bears. At the column's base are Roman capital letters, which were first painted and then carved into the stone with a chisel.

Twombly's capitals-only typeface became an unprecedented hit in the movie business, a grower that eventually became a Hollywood cliché. Over the past two decades it has been used regularly on posters and packaging for everything from the all-conquering *Titanic*, via *A Beautiful Mind*, to *The Last Samurai* and *Nancy Drew*. The television series *The West Wing* used Trajan, as did an ITV adaptation of Jane Austen's *Northanger Abbey*.

Trajan is nevertheless widely admired for its elegance and its respectful evocation of a classical form. Twombly went on to design or co-design several more typefaces, including Adobe Caslon (see page 20) and Chaparral, before leaving Adobe, and the world of type design, in the early 2000s.

A giant billboard overlooking Sunset Boulevard, Los Angeles, advertises the re-release in 3-D of James Cameron's *Titanic*, 2012. You can spot the seriffed Trajan relatively easily by the absence of serifs on the top-left and bottom-right corners of the 'N', the little gap in the 'P' and the extravagant 'Q'.

ABCDEF123
LMPQ,.£%

SCALA
Digital grows up quickly

1991
Martin Majoor

Scala is often referred to as the first 'serious' typeface from FontShop's FontFont stable of innovative digital typefaces. Its origins were bespoke and practical – in the late 1980s Martin Majoor (1960–) was an in-house designer for the Vredenburg Music Centre in Utrecht, so he designed a typeface that would meet a wide variety of needs, from posters to detailed classical concert programmes, much of it produced in-house using newly acquired Apple Macintosh computers.

Majoor had experienced the limitations of producing digital typefaces while working for hardware manufacturer Océ, and the challenge of making a versatile typeface resulted in a hard-working, adaptable book face. (He had previously studied at the Arnhem Academy, where his near contemporaries included fellow type designers Fred Smeijers and Evert Bloemsma.)

Scala included small caps and non-lining figures as well as other typographical niceties not found among many of the new typefaces of that time, so it quickly found favour with book and newspaper designers: it was adopted by the German publisher Taschen and the Dutch daily *Algemeen Dagblad*.

Enthusiastic early adopters included writer-designers Robin Kinross and the duo of Ellen Lupton and Abbott Miller, who used Scala in their fascinating book *Design Writing Research: Writing about Graphic Design* (1996). Lupton writes approvingly of Scala's 'crisp geometry and humanist references' and its 'unfashionably bottom-heavy x-height', while Stephen Coles calls it an 'old-style serif for the digital world.'

A page from the book *The Bathroom, the Kitchen and the Aesthetics of Waste*, designed and written by J. Abbott Miller and Ellen Lupton and typeset in Martin Majoor's crystal-clear digital serif typeface Scala (body text) and Gill Sans (captions).

abcdefghij123
LMNO,.£%*

In this 1934 ad for Armstrong Linoleum Floors, the unusual hoop design of the bench and the streamline banding around the tub announce the vanguard styling of this fashion-conscious flooring material.

16. Catherine Wooley, "The Bathroom— A Developed Interior," *House Beautiful* (February 1932): 125-126.

Whereas the modern bathroom was once valued for its intensified standards of cleanliness, these standards now informed other areas of domestic life. The bathroom, formerly positioned as a kind of hospital-within-the-home, was now being re-absorbed into the fabric of the house, subject to the same decorative attention as other rooms. A 1932 article began with a scenario suggestive of a definitive shift: "When Mr. and Mrs. Jebediah Jones built their brand new house some five years ago, their bathroom—white of tile, glistening as the inside of a new refrigerator—was the acme of hygienic perfection.... But when [her] younger sister Jessie displayed *her* new house the other day, the bathroom turned out to have fixtures of Copenhagen blue,...a dark green lacquered floor, ...and a shower curtain of apricot."[16] Consumers were being encouraged to soften and personalize the industrial aesthetic of the bathroom.

The decorated bathroom was spurred by the appearance of color bathroom fixtures in the late 1920s. The Universal Sanitary Manufacturing Company was the first to introduce colored fixtures, followed by Kohler and Crane in 1928, and Standard in the early 1930s (Winkler 22). Initially featuring light pastels, manufacturers later introduced deep colors, including a black ensemble by Kohler. Colored fixtures dominated bathroom advertising, but were not widely accepted until the 1950s. This may have been due to their cost—which ads described as "just pennies more"—but also reflected the endurance of whiteness as an ideal of hygiene.

A 1935 ad for Carrara Structural Steel Glass Walls features the rounded corners, round "porthole" mirror, and horizontality of streamlined design.

META
Here comes the Meta man

1991
Erik Spiekermann

There was a moment, for a few years before and after the turn of the millennium, when Meta attained a certain omnipresence. Erik Spiekermann's creation became the typeface that could do anything, from architectural magazines to compilations of classical music – used small for captions or big for advertising.

Meta had a lengthy and contested gestation: the typeface began as a commission for the Deutsche Bundespost (German Post Office), which was then Europe's biggest employer, with more than half a million on the payroll. The concept for the typeface, originally known as PT, was that it would remain legible even when badly printed on cheap paper at small sizes. However, Spiekermann (1947–) rejected the branded blandness of most contemporary sans serifs – he wanted the typeface to be both neutral and unmistakable, 'the complete antithesis of Helvetica'.

Spiekermann's design method was analytical – he and his colleagues looked at six different type families to see what they had in common, and they created a typeface in three weights. The Bundespost, however, cancelled the job at a late stage, worried that such a change from Helvetica might 'cause unrest'. Spiekermann took PT with him to his new company MetaDesign, which used it as its corporate typeface, named Meta Bleifrei.

Spiekermann founded the digital font distribution company FontShop in 1989, with Joan Spiekermann (then his wife) and Neville Brody. When FontShop started its own digital type library, FontFont, in 1991, they released the typeface, now renamed FF Meta, and it quickly became (and remains) FontFont's best seller.

Poster designed by Erik Spiekermann for PUBLIC, a bicycle company in San Francisco, 2012. The client's brief was to 'interpret the concept of "public" with a vision to reclaim urban streets'.

abcdefgh123
IJKLM,.£%*"

PUBLIC

space | enemy | park | toilet | radio
access | view | entrance | building
baths | company | enterprise | deal
transport | information | opinion
money | private partnership | pool
utility | relations | surplus | library
storage | gardens | passage | vote
performance | works | playground
announcement | school | crossing
grounds | beach | records | transit
housing | data | declaration | issue
parking | train | bicycles | persona
institution | address | appearance

BLUR
In and out of focus

1991
Neville Brody for
FontFont

Come the hour, come the typeface. Blur was the quintessential early-1990s typeface. Designer Neville Brody (1957–), well known for his art direction of style magazines *The Face* and *Arena* during the 1980s, had always bent display typefaces to his will or drawn new ones when they were needed. Brody took the forms of an existing typeface (thought to be AG Old Face) and subjected them to process: creating vector images from blurred greyscale images of the font.

Such transformations were not new. Examples of distorted and blurred type abound within graphic design: Robert Massin printed on condoms to stretch type; Robert Brownjohn projected letters on to a woman's skin for his *Goldfinger* movie titles. But these were bespoke applications. The new desktop technology of font manipulation software gave the process a new, practical twist: Blur was a typeface that anyone could buy and then use to give their work a Brody-esque edge.

Brody was a partner (with Joan and Erik Spiekermann) in FontShop and the foundry's 'label', FontFont, and FF Blur quickly became one of its most popular digital typefaces. Two decades on, Blur still gets plenty of use, but while nightclubs might appreciate its rave-era associations, soft drinks manufacturers appear to value its essential fuzziness.

The concept of communicating through blurred type lives on, however, in Wolff Olins's branding for the various Tate galleries, whose deliberately unfocused logos remain highly effective.

A flyer promoting a jazz festival in Berlin, 1994.

abcdefghi123
JKLMNO,.£%⭑

JazzFest Berlin '94

präsentiert von der Berliner Sparkasse

16. bis 20.11.

HAUS DER
KULTUREN
DER WELT

Berliner Sparkasse
Abteilung der LandesBank Berlin

Köstritzer
Schwarzbier

COMIC SANS
No joke

1994
Vincent Connare
for Microsoft

In retrospect it seems extraordinary that Vincent Connare's simple problem-solving type design for a CD-ROM game, commissioned for Microsoft, should have become one of the most overused and most talked-about typefaces, spawning hate sites, ironic applications (the 'happy' app that changes the type of any website, however sober, into Comic Sans) and a legion of jokes. Yet it remains one of the few typefaces that non-designers argue about. Or talk about at all.

The typeface's popularity and notoriety is also a product of timing: it appeared on a million PCs when there were few 'friendly' typefaces with which to laser-print school fête and 'lost pet' notices. This was an era during which the process of selecting typefaces underwent a seismic shift. Formerly the domain of a professional cabal (designers, printers, etc.), font choice became an everyday task for individual computer owners worldwide.

In the 1990s Vincent Connare (1960–) was an in-house designer at Microsoft (where his other designs included Trebuchet MS and Webdings). He noticed that the interface for the children's software package Microsoft Bob had carefully coded comic characters whose speech bubbles 'spoke' in Times New Roman. Connare thought that was laughably inappropriate and quickly devised a new font based on comic-book lettering. Though Comic Sans wasn't actually used for Bob, the typeface was later incorporated into a version of Windows 95 as a system font.

For many people seeking to write an informal memo or note on their PC, Comic Sans became an easy choice: friendly, legible and free. Today, this typeface can also be spotted on signage, shop fronts and cash mashines.

abcdefgh12
IJKL,.£%*

ALTHOUGH WE ARE SWEET AND CUTE PLEASE REMEMBER THAT WE DO HAVE TEETH!

EMERGENCY EXIT

SALEM-KEIZER PUBLIC SCHOOLS
209

RIKTIGE LEKER

ed. univ. et med. dent.

MEDIZINALRAT

R. GERHARD TASCHNER

EINGANG UM DIE ECKE
HANAUSKAGASSE 4

Andén Sin Servicio

his AIM will charge up to
75 for LINK debit card cash
withdrawals

DO NOT REMOVE CARD
UNTIL INSTRUCTED

TRM
LAU
EPK

D PÅ 3 BOKSTÄVER

099 - 317 17

GEORGIA
A font finds its ecological niche

1996
Matthew Carter
for Microsoft

Georgia is one of the most frequently seen typefaces on the planet, and is completely free, tireless, efficient and elegantly legible to all manner of people who typically have little interest in type. It can be seen on millions of screens, from smartphones to office monitors, every hour of every day.

Microsoft commissioned Carter (1937–) to make Georgia as a seriffed companion to the equally hard-working sans-serif Verdana (also 1996). The software giant made both typefaces freely available in the interests of improved onscreen legibility.

Georgia is easy on the eye, quiet and strong, without being bland or mannered, and benefits from being 'screen-first'. As with his masterly design of Bell Centennial (see page 86), Carter attacked the challenge from first principles. Yet, in comparison to earlier typefaces that Carter had designed to cope with bleeding edge technology (such as CRT Gothic, cleverly engineered to work on now-obsolete cathode ray tube screens), Georgia has withstood the test of time.

At first, Carter was reluctant to design another 'problem-solving' typeface, worried that it would soon make itself obsolete. He recalls: 'Microsoft replied that the resolution of monitor screens was stuck and would not improve significantly for at least ten years … and I took on the job. Microsoft's prediction has been pretty accurate … Verdana and Georgia have had an opportunity to establish an ecological niche in the typographic world.' Carter also recalls that, at the time, he was also working on Miller, a typeface family based on Scotch Roman, and that the Scotch influence probably rubbed off on Georgia.

Georgia – a truly worldwide font. Website for Wright & Wright Architects, London (top); the online edition of the *National Post*, a Canadian newspaper founded in 1998, and slaveryfootprint.org, a website that visualizes the use of forced labour in the manufacture of consumer goods.

abcdefgh123 LMNO,.£%"

Wright & Wright is an award-winning architectural practice
based in London. Formed in 1994, the practice has built a strong
portfolio of projects in the UK for prestigious clients in the cultural,
education, housing and office sectors. A key element of the practice's
work focuses on developing designs to support those with a range
of special needs. All projects are underpinned by a commitment to
delivering the highest quality buildings and to supporting clients
through every stage and aspect of a project.

Corpus Christi College
Cambridge

"Wright & Wright's sleight of hand makes
hard things look effortless as they devise
ingenious ways to use, transform and
connect pockets of space"

Cathy Slessor
Architectural Review

How many slaves

work for you?

What?   Find out
Slaves work for me?   Take the survey

↓   →

GOTHAM
Letters of hope

2000
Tobias Frere-Jones
(with Jesse Ragan) for
Hoefler & Frere-Jones

Gotham, based on public display lettering found on the streets of New York City, came into its own when it was selected for Barack Obama's successful 2008 campaign for the US Presidency, its confident capital 'O' dominating badges, website banners and the famous series of posters designed by Shepard Fairey: the word 'HOPE' looks especially convincing set in Gotham.

Gotham, originally designed for *GQ* magazine, first acquired fame when it was inscribed into a slab of granite in the foundations of New York's Freedom Tower on the site of the World Trade Center. Tobias Frere-Jones (1970–) is an aficionado of the city's 'non-typographic lettering', the industrial signs and nameplates that he has observed and photographed over the years. Gotham is not directly related to any sign in particular, but it has an urban toughness that has found many uses (and many imitators). 'We do projects that are taught by history rather than transcribing it,' said Frere-Jones to design writer Alice Twemlow.

Hoefler & Frere-Jones is among the most technically accomplished and commercially driven of the twenty-first-century foundries, producing typefaces such as the sans-serif Verlag (originally made for the Guggenheim Museum) and the 32-strong family Knockout, making many typefaces for magazine and newspaper clients. The 2012 Presidential race between Obama and Republican challenger, Mitt Romney, became an 'all H&F-J' election, with both parties using typefaces from the company.

'Hope' poster by Shepard Fairey, 2008, one of the posters that came to symbolize the optimism of Barack Obama's first presidential campaign.

abcdefg123
LMNO,.£%"

GUARDIAN EGYPTIAN
Future-proof family

2005–
Paul Barnes and
Christian Schwartz
(Commercial Type)

When creative director Mark Porter commissioned Paul Barnes and Christian Schwartz to design a typeface for a new-look, new-size incarnation of the UK newspaper *The Guardian*, their design partnership was a virtual one, conducted by phone and email. The first time that Barnes and Schwartz met in person was at Heathrow airport, several months into the project.

The Guardian redesign required a typeface family with a large number of weights and sizes, from the smallest types (agates) required for the sports results to the fattest display headlines; it had to be legible and adaptable across a range of sections, and it had to signal newness with a different tone of voice. 'If everyone else is shouting louder and louder, the only way you can be heard is by talking in a normal tone of voice – or even whispering,' says Porter, who supervised 'the conception and birth' of the typeface.

Barnes and Schwartz took inspiration from the Egyptian faces of mid-nineteenth-century Britain (see pages 32–35), but came up with a far-reaching (and multi-award-winning) type design system that is entirely of the twenty-first.

Along with a select group of designers of a similar generation (including Hoefler & Frere-Jones and Henrik Kubel of A2/SW/HK), the duo of Paul Barnes (1970–) and Christian Schwartz (1977–), now operating as Commercial Type, has become one of the most influential type teams of the early twenty-first century. Between them, Barnes and Schwartz have produced a large variety of big type families, including some significant revivals.

The Guardian Egyptian family now has more than 200 fonts, including an extensive sans-serif version. The typeface has also adapted well to new products launched by *The Guardian*, including its app for the iPad.

abcdefghij12
LMNO,.£%;.

Boris caught in a bicycle crash of an interview

Cyprus told: take bank levy or leave euro

Funding lifeline to be cut off today

Panic at €100 cash machine limit

No evidence Berezovsky was killed say police

Berezovsky death

iPad edition

theguardian

Sport Motor racing
Webber and Vettel at war

World

Financial

In pictures

UBUNTU

2011
Dalton Maag

The Ubuntu family has not yet changed the world, but it aspires to make a global difference. Type books and magazines tend to be dominated by the 52 characters of what typographers call the 'Latin alphabet'. Though great type designers have long tackled the challenges of type for the world's myriad tongues, financial, cultural and technical limitations have resulted in type for non-Latin alphabets being marginalized or ignored completely. At the dawn of the digital revolution, things got worse. Where cases of metal type could hold around 300 'sorts', and casters like the Monotype could swap matrices for use in different countries, the computer keyboard was limited by ASCII code that handled just 94 printable characters. This made setting Eastern European languages difficult, let alone words in the other major script groups – Greek, Cyrillic, Hebrew, Arabic and beyond.

Happily, the rapid evolution of digital type has begun to liberate type for other languages, and there is a system called Unicode (founded 1991), effectively an 'United Nations of Type', that assigns numbers for up to 1,114,112 characters, enough to cover every language – living or dead – in the world.

Ubuntu's makers would like it eventually to become a truly global typeface. But perhaps the most radical aspect of its design is that Ubuntu was released under an 'open source' licence: anyone can make their own version, or add new characters based on Ubuntu's DNA. Democracy or free-for-all? These are early days for open-source typefaces. We may one day see as many variations on Ubuntu as there were scribes in the days before Gutenberg.

Ubuntu has the utopian aim of its being freely available to anyone in the world, in any technology, and in more than 200 languages.

abcdefg123
LMNO,.£%;.

GLOSSARY

blackletter A general term for the heavy script typefaces used by Gutenberg (derived from handwriting with a broad-nibbed pen). Major variants include Textura, Fraktur and Rotunda.

broken script See blackletter.

counter The space inside letters, whether closed (in 'a or 'g') or partly open ('n' or 'u').

diacritics Marks added to letters that indicate different speech sounds, also known as accents.

display face Type intended for use at large sizes (newspaper headlines, advertising slogans) rather than for text setting.

font Not interchangeable with typeface. Originally the smallest saleable unit of a typeface – a consignment of cold metal ('I purchased a font of ten point Helvetica') but in the digital age the distinctions have evolved: if typefaces are songs, then fonts are downloads – the method of delivery ('All these fonts came free with my laptop's operating system').

foundry, letter-founder, etc. The company or person that manufactures or otherwise makes and sells typefaces.

italic Used to distinguish certain elements (works of art, foreign words) in a text. The sloping design of italic characters has its roots in handwriting, and some characters, such as the 'g', can be quite different from the roman. In typefaces for which no italic exists (such as DM Schulbuch, used throughout this book), an 'artificial' slope has been applied by the page layout program. See roman.

hand-setting Setting out lines of characters and spaces – actual physical type – by hand. See letterpress.

hot metal Mechanized casters such as the Monotype and Linotype machines produced freshly cast type from molten metal.

letterpress Printing by (literally) pressing inked type on to paper. Once the dominant mode of printing, but now largely replaced by cheaper methods such as offset litho and digital printing.

lower case Typographer's word for small (minuscule) letters. The term comes from the printer's custom of storing type in wooden cases – the upper was used for capitals (majuscule); the lower for small letters.

matrix The metal part that bears the strike from the punch; i.e. the negative impression of a character from which printing type can be cast.

nameplate The form in which the title of a newspaper or magazine is presented – usually on the front page.

offset litho The dominant form of commercial printing from the 1960s to the 2010s.

photosetting Typesetting that uses photographic characters instead of metal type; in common use from the 1950s to the 1980s.

punchcutter The person who cut letterforms into the punch that stamped the matrix.

roman Neither blackletter nor italic. The most common form for text typefaces since the early sixteenth century. A term often used to distinguish a typeface design from its italic or weight variants.

router A machine that carves shapes, used for the production of wood type since the nineteenth century.

sans serif Without serifs.

serif The little marks – 'feet' – that may grace the ends of strokes in characters of serif typefaces.

typeface The design of a set of characters. See font.

typesetting The art of setting words in type to be printed (or viewed onscreen) later.

typographer A skilled person who lays out type. Not to be confused with ' type designer', a person who designs typefaces.

upper case Typographer's word for capital letters (majuscule). See lower case.

INDEX

PICTURE CREDITS

CREDITS

An Hachette UK Company
www.hachette.co.uk

First published in Great
Britain in 2013 by
Conran Octopus Ltd
in association with
The Design Museum

Conran Octopus Ltd,
a division of Octopus
Publishing Group Ltd
Endeavour House
189 Shaftesbury Avenue
London WC2H 8JY
www.octopusbooks.co.uk
www.octopusbooksusa.com

Text copyright © Octopus
Publishing Group Ltd 2013
Design and layout
copyright © Octopus
Publishing Group Ltd 2013

Distributed in the US by
Hachette Book Group USA
237 Park Avenue
New York NY 10017 USA

Distributed in Canada by
Canadian Manda Group
165 Dufferin Street
Toronto, Ontario, Canada
M6K 3H6

A CIP catalogue record for
this book is available from
the British Library

Text written by:
John L Walters

Publisher:
Alison Starling
Consultant Editor:
Deyan Sudjic
Editors:
Alex Stetter and Katy Denny
Copy Editor:
Robert Anderson

Art Director:
Jonathan Christie
Design:
Untitled
Picture Research:
Anne-Marie Hoines

*Assistant Production
Manager:*
Caroline Alberti

ISBN 978 1 84091 629 4
Printed and bound in China